WHERE DID MY PEOPLE GO?
GRANDMOTHER'S STORY

AKIIKI DAISY KABAGARAMA

Where Did My People Go? Grandmother's Story

Copyright © 2019 Akiiki Daisy Kabagarama

All rights reserved. No part of this publication may be reproduced, distributed, or transmitted in any form or by any means, including photocopying, recording, or other electronic or mechanical methods, without the prior written permission of the copyright holder.

Cover design, book design and layout by D. Shawn Carter

Library of Congress Control Number: 2019955621
International Standard Book Number: 978-0-578-60359-9
Printed in the United States of America by Mennonite Press, Inc., Newton, Kansas. *www.MennonitePress.com*

ACKNOWLEDGEMENTS

In all my previous writing projects, I have not had such a long list of people to thank for offering me support. The list of acknowledgements this time is almost equivalent to a separate chapter. This is no surprise because I have never written a book like this one. Bringing forth a story that began in the 1880s needed many hands, shoulders and prayers to lift it up.

First and foremost, I am very thankful to God for giving me the vision, inspiration, determination and ability to tell this story. Whenever I got tempted to give up due to strong "winds" that were blowing or when doubt arose, I heard God say: "You are not alone. I am with you."

A big "Thank You" to Mukaaka, my Grandmother for selecting me from all her children and grandchildren to tell her amazing story. In many ways, she demonstrated to me that I was the child that she called "Owangwire ha mukono" which is translated as "The one who fell on my arm."

Mukaaka gave me a big responsibility from early childhood that drove me and gave me direction in life. She taught me how to rise above limitations; build an extended family; have compassion and get up from a fall. She also kept me rooted in my culture. She was my mentor, guardian, friend, confidant and my faith-builder. Mukaaka pointed me to God as my anchor who would never fail me no matter what came my way. She taught me how to pray and expect an answer.

I am very grateful to King Daudi Kasagama Kyebambe IV who ruled Tooro from 1891 to 1928. His kind act of raising my grandmother made it possible for me to exist. Without her surviving and learning how to be an excellent parent and leader, my mother and her siblings would not have made it in life. I would not be here to have children of my own and to tell this story.

I am very grateful to my mother Ateenyi for giving me the fundamental tools to accomplish this task. From early on in life, she showed me the value of education. She provided for me materially; coached me as a teacher; taught me how to read and write; showed me how to cross barriers; gave me courage and above all, kept me in church.

My mother was not afraid to go where no one else in her family had gone before. Without saying it directly, she taught me how to be a trailblazer and to pursue my goals, even though this meant standing alone, sometimes. Not once, did I hear my mother complain about the heavy responsibility she carried raising me and my siblings as a single mother.

I appreciate my father, brothers, sisters, aunts, uncles and grandparents from the Bagaya extended family. As I researched information about Tooro history, I became increasingly proud of my roots in Mwenge. I was particularly impressed to find out that the school to provide education for Tooro royalty was based in Mwenge. I am also appreciative of my father for his teaching profession. Having a father and a mother who were educators helped shape my love for learning and becoming an educator myself.

I am also very grateful to my Aunt Akiiki, Aunt Amooti and Uncle Apuuli, my mother's siblings. They demonstrated to me the power of love, unity, determination, faith and hard work in creating a successful family. They were all "Batembuzi" or pioneers who without fear, explored new territories.

Mukaaka's children all loved their mother dearly and cared for her. They also protected one another and helped raise each other's children. I will always be grateful to my uncle who gave me his precious iron when I was leaving home for boarding school. Besides keeping my school uniform orderly and tidy, the iron earned me many friends and made me popular at school. I remember many Saturday afternoons in boarding school when students who had no irons of their own lined up to borrow mine.

Although for the past thirty-seven years I have lived away from my siblings in Tooro, I have always felt their presence. I remember our home with great love and affection. I am so glad that we were touched and held by Mukaaka's hands. Even those who are no longer with us today experienced the richness of life through our incredible ancestor. Her legacy lives on through our children and generations to come.

Without the love, support and prayers of my entire

family here in the United States, this work would have been next to impossible. For a very long time, I did not want to share this part of our family history with my children. I wanted to leave this "Ihano" or mystery alone. My fear was that it would make them sad and depressed. I thought I had come to the new land for a fresh start, not to dig up the past. Was I wrong!! Ever since I told my children about Mukaaka's story, they have been longing to know more about her.

My children pushed me, gave advice, read the first draft and told me that this book was too important to ignore. They urged me to allow Mukaaka's voice to be heard. I can tell that even my grandchildren are longing to be taught about our family history and culture. From these young people, I have confirmed what brought me to the United States of America. I came to experience freedom. This encompasses learning from my past, utilizing opportunities in the present and building for the future. In this book, I have attained my " American Dream."

Many thanks go to my husband, partner and co-parent of many years. He has stood by me in winter, summer and all the other seasons. As he shared his own family stories of tragedy and triumph, I was encouraged to move forward with Mukaaka's story. I am particularly grateful to him for believing me when I decided to transfer Mukaaka's body from Burungu to Nyabukara. Had he declared this task to be impossible, it would have become so. I was convinced he knew deep inside that I would accomplish this seemingly-impossible task.

Many thanks go to my teachers at every level of education who nurtured my love and enthusiasm for learning. They provided me the right environment to become a life-long learner. In primary school when Mother moved away from home to teach at distant schools, my teachers adopted me as their own child. They instilled in me principles of hard work, self-determination, discipline, honesty and pursuit of higher goals. They recognized my talents and tried their best to develop them.

Many thanks go to Uganda, my country of birth and the Ugandan people. This glorious land of beautiful people gave me the opportunity to grow and thrive. It is in Uganda that my eyes were opened to the world through education. When I moved away from the comfort of Tooro to explore higher education in Ankole and Buganda districts, I felt at home. The excellent education that I received at Makerere University prepared me well to face a world of challenges and opportunities.

A big tribute goes to the African American Institute that awarded me a scholarship to pursue further education in the United States of America. By partnering with Iowa State University, I was afforded an excellent education. I also received adequate financial sustenance while pursuing my studies. This act of generosity freed me to pay maximum attention to my education. The door that they opened helped to make the writing of this book possible, many years later.

Thanks to the many people who welcomed me to the United States and provided me a home away from home.

These include professors, students, and religious communities. When I decided to launch my teaching career, Sandy Beverly of Salina, Kansas took me in not only as a co-worker but as a sister. She opened a new chapter in my life.

Sandy Beverly made me understand this nation in a unique and personal way. I felt my identity changing from that of a stranger or visitor to someone who belongs. Through her kind act and hospitality, I got to know wonderful people such as the Gordon family and many others. It is in the church to which Sandy introduced me that I first announced my call into ministry.

Because of Sandy's welcoming attitude, my family got extended and enriched. We became as "American as Apple Pie !!!" Our family was able to explore and understand the American traditions such as Thanksgiving. Sandy introduced us to her delicious Macaroni and Cheese, plus corn bread. The Thanksgiving Turkey that we had named "The Big Bird" got transformed into very delicious and tasty food. From her and Mother Cora, I learned how to make my own version of turkey that up to this day has attracted our children's friends to Thanksgiving dinner in our home.

I am also very grateful to Stephen Kaboyo Araali and Felly Kaboyo Akiiki of Tooro. We first met on the campus of McPherson College and instantly became family. It was a breath of fresh air for me to keep my connections with Tooro and to speak Rutooro in mid-America. When I was introduced to the Nyakatura family, my joy got multiplied. They were present at the preaching of my first sermon. A few years later, I met Patience Kaboyo Abwoli who made a wonderful addition to the family.

When the Tooro America Association (TAA) was formed, I was invited to speak at the organization's conference. Speaking to a large assembly of Batooro was a very transforming experience for me. They understood my comedy and poetry and I was instantly named "The Maya Angelou of Tooro." This honor made me even more determined to write this book. I knew it would be relevant, appreciated and valued.

I am grateful to the people of Wichita, Kansas who for more than twenty years have called me. "Dr. Daisy." I take it as a sign of respect, love and a term of endearment. I have known all along that this tittle is beyond academic achievement. I feel that this community has sensed that I am carrying something precious within me. They have given me permission to be a "healer." They have also revived my title of "Owagonza Abantu" meaning "One who Loves People." The elders gave me this title when I was a child, growing up in Burungu Village.

Thanks to the two elders of Wichita, Mrs Blanche Childers and Mrs Addie Pearson who adopted me into their families as their own daughter. As I type their names, I can feel their presence. The love and prayers they gave to me have sustained me through the years. Even though they are departed from this earth, they have never gone from my heart. By adopting me as their daughter, they confirmed what Mukaaka always told me. She undoubtedly convinced me that I have relatives all over the world.

Thanks to Loveness Mpanje for her love and support. Her entire family is part of my extended family that helped usher in this book.

I appreciate all the searchers for truth and knowledge who have held my hand, welcomed me and valued my perspective that is different from most. I would like to mention, in particular, Dr. Dorothy Billings, Dr. Hubert Brown and Professor Tony Brown. These and many other colleagues have welcomed me into their debate circles and appreciated what I brought to the table. They have helped me reach the conclusion that Mukaaka's story is part and parcel of the academic discourse.

I would like to express special thanks to the members of the Wichita African Union. They listened to the Drum's call and responded to the Drumbeat when I called on them for unity. Their enthusiasm offered me a relevant context in which to tell this story. Deep inside, I knew they would value this book and see the story as their own. My appreciation also goes to other Africans both at home and in the diaspora. While working on this book, I could imagine them inviting their children, family and friends to read this story. I could hear them say, "Her grandmother sounds like my own grandmother and her village is like mine. O My God!!!"

My very deep gratitude goes to the Onijala family. They welcomed my family to Wichita over twenty years ago. In their unique way, they gave me the support needed to write this book.

Many thanks go to the people whose patience and

technical skills helped me accomplish the task of writing this book. When I first met Gina Laiso of Mennonite Press, I had no doubt that she had great interest in my work. She was determined to have it published and to give Mukaaka a voice. Whenever I needed an extension, she gladly accepted and never gave up on me. I had a feeling that she was always at the other end of the phone, waiting to hear from me. She truly helped me "birth" this book.

I am also very grateful to other staff of Mennonite Press. Shawn Carter's enthusiasm kept me going. His great sense of imagination and creativity brought forth a very beautiful book that transports the reader to witness Mukaaka's life. Thanks also to Karen Siemens for her welcoming spirit and support. This is my third book to be published by Mennonite Press. Her commitment has been unwavering.

My heartfelt thanks go to Wendy Pope for the editorial work on the manuscript. Her probing, patience and professionalism helped produce the excellent book that we are all enjoying. She was able to quickly immerse herself in another culture and provide the necessary guidance, unhindered by new expressions and names. I appreciated her sense of curiosity when she wanted to know the meanings of Empaako of the Batooro people.

Many thanks go to Joel Mtebe who I often tell, "You can do anything." He joined my team with great enthusiasm, technical ability and a host of other skills. He was available both day and night to make sure that this book became complete. He researched photographs, perfected them and made sure they complemented the story very well. He took on the project as his very own.

I also called on Joel to do formatting work and many other tasks. He always respected me as his elder and addressed me as "Auntie." As a result, I felt protected, appreciated and cared for. His behavior toward me transported me back to Africa where the elders are revered.

Joel's attitude toward me and this book project gave me the urgency and obligation to do the work and complete the task that was set before me. I am also very grateful to his wife Moureen for supporting this work one hundred percent. Whenever I felt hungry and missed traditional food, I could always rely on her to come to my rescue with chapati, pilao, kuku, dodo and mandaazi. Her constant smile and gentle spirit gave me the calm air to keep on doing the work.

A big "Thank You" to my sister from Burungu Lillian Kairumba Carvalho Adyeri for her great support of this work. Since December of 2017 when I shared the vision with her, she has been running the race at full speed. Every time I turned around, I saw some cultural information, historical data, words of encouragement, prayer, music or photographs from her to sustain me and to complement this work. She never got tired of my questions. Her responses were always timely and accurate. I call her the "God Mother" of this book.

Lillian Adyeri often reminds me of her mother, our Mama Abwoli who made sure I drank some milk and ate snacks from home whenever she paid a visit to her daughter who was in boarding school with me. Whenever I saw their family car pull up in the school compound, I ran fast to get my share of delicacies from home.

Often, Lillian and I marvel at God's goodness for protecting us and enabling us to work together on this book. As far as we know, we are the only two people who grew up together in Burungu and now reside in the United States of America. It is wonderful to know and work with someone who knew Mukaaka and my entire family very well.

Through Lillian's connections, I have re-lived the kindness and generosity of the Tooro people. I have experienced afresh the "Amakune" and "Ak'Obuntu" of the people who raised me. The word "Amakune" can be described as having good character that is a combination of grace, kindness, hospitality and a giving heart. "Ak'Obuntu" can be summarized as "Human Essence or Goodness."

The people who are associated with Karuziika (the Palace) offered me very valuable information about Mukaaka's story. One of these people is Reverend Canon Rubaale Araali. When he shared with me excerpts from his 1975 master's degree thesis, I was able to verify the "Rwabudongo" battle of 1893. It is during this battle that Mukaaka's entire family had vanished.

Reverend Rubaale also provided vital information regarding Tooro history and Palace culture. He is the one who told me that Mukaaka and other ladies at Karuziika were known as "Banyaanya" or Sisters of the King. I shed tears of Joy when he told me that he had personally met precious Mukaaka face-to-face.

I am very grateful to the people who welcomed me

to Uganda, my homeland in January of 2006. I returned home after living away for twenty-four years. The anxiety I carried within me turned into joy when my family members met me at Entebbe Airport. I was also grateful when Mr. Stephen Kaboyo Araali invited me and other guests from the United States to visit the Tooro headquarters and his home in Kampala.

My visit to Kasubi Royal Tombs with Princess Bagaaya Akiiki ignited a fire within me, urging me to write this book as quickly as possible. It was a big honor to walk with our very valuable Princess who has made Tooro and Uganda very proud in many ways.

Many thanks go to Mr. Charles Mawenu Araali and Reverend Joram Musana Araali. The two gentlemen drove and walked long distances to conduct research with the elders. Among these elders is Reverend Baguma Adyeri and Mr. Charles Muhanga Araali. Besides conducting interviews, Reverend Musana took most of the photographs in this book.

To all of you, I am saying:" *Mwebale muno Abarungi. Mukama Abongere Emigisa*" *that is*" *Thank you very much, Good People. May God Give You more Blessings*"

THE DRUMBEAT

The drumbeat calling you and me
to dance to the tune of love,
to the rhythm of life.
The drum calls us to gather in unity.
It is time to pray, eat
And celebrate our being.
The drum calls everyone to remember
Those heroes, both present and gone,
Those very bones that give us form,
Those very souls that keep us informed
Of who we are and where we are.
The drum tells us to put aside our fears,
To join the dance with a joyful spirit.
The sound brings the past,
Shows the present,
and beckons the future.
The notes are simple, the melody is sweet,
Sounding our ancestors' secret dreams.

Akiiki D. Kabagarama,
February 2. 2013

WHERE DID MY PEOPLE GO?

PREFACE

Welcome to a book about my grandmother's life. You will encounter an amazing woman who overcame amazing hurdles to rise to prominence among her people. She lost her entire family in the 1893 Rwabudongo battle between Kings Kabalega of Bunyoro and Kyebambe 1V of Tooro. King Kyebambe gave my grandmother and other battle survivors a fresh start in life. He adopted them into his family.

This story is from the time I got to know Grandmother (Mukaaka) at around the age of three until she departed in 1971. At age three, I came to an understanding that I was under her care. I was starting to speak and did not pronounce some words correctly. I remember Cousin Byaruhanga teasing me by imitating how I said the verb "to eat." Instead of saying "kulya", I pronounced it as "akuya."

At about five years of age, I began to understand that Mukaaka had a very important story. She told it to me often and it made her very sad. At about that time, I started writing in the dust of my home compound with my finger as a pen. I also created characters in my mind that I often conversed with. This was the beginning of my love for writing and storytelling. I must have been trying to communicate with my departed ancestors that Mukaaka often talked about. Since then, I have used different writing methods, progressing from writing with a finger in the dust, to a stick on a banana leaf, a pencil on a piece of paper, a pen in a notebook, a typewriter and finally, a computer. It has been quite a journey!!

It has taken me a long time before gaining the courage to write this book. I have shed tears, felt pain and also experienced tremendous joy upon reflecting on the role Mukaaka played in raising me. I have told her story in poetry and short stories over the decades, particularly after migrating from Uganda to the United States. It was too painful for me to write the entire story.

Mukaaka often spoke to me in the following words: "They were taken from my heart. I was about six years of age, a few feet tall. They all disappeared. I was left alone. My two sisters and I took off running, dodging snakes, crocodiles and other dangerous creatures. One of my sisters died on the way. She was bitten by a poisonous snake. After covering her boy with what we could find, the two of us kept on running. Eventually, we met other people who were running. We joined them on the journey to nowhere. We were running away from danger. The captors, known as Abarusura, were still around. We journeyed on until the king's forces came to our rescue.

I do not remember how long we ran before the king's soldiers came to our rescue. All I know is that I was exhausted. I remember the older people among us clapping their hands when they saw the soldiers (Abaserukali b'Omukama). The king that I call Kabumba (the Potter) took us in. I know the time. I can remember it well. It was known as: "Kusingwa Kwa Rwabudongo." Rwabudongo and Ireeta were the leaders of the invading army. They took away my people. Up to now, I ask myself: "Where did my people go?" (She stops and sobs). I draw my comfort from God. I constantly sing; "Nserra abantu baange. Abantu bakamburaho ira." The song is translated as "I am looking for my people. My people disappeared from me a long time ago."

I am convinced that my people will one day return to me. Every day, I ask the mighty river, the lakes and all the streams to help me find my people. I seek help from the forests and ask the animals in the wild to help me in the search. I call the village elders to beat the drum and ask them never to give up hope. Child (looking at me) never forget these words. Wherever you go, search for our people."

These are the words I constantly heard from my grandmother (Mukaaka). In public, she was very strong and brave, trying hard to protect her family. She was the matriarch who kept alert all the time, attempting to ward off danger. I was young then, very young. Although I did not fully comprehend my grandmother's life story, I could feel her pain. For some unique reason which I now call divine, my grandmother chose me to be her confidant, friend and comforter.

Many decades have passed yet I still remember the story as though I heard it yesterday. For a long time, I attempted to share this tragedy that so profoundly impacted my family. I had no success until now. Although I do not entertain procrastination, in this case, I found no courage to tell Mukaaka's life story. The pain was over-bearing, at times. Whenever I got out a pen to write the full story, I got a sharp stomach ache and experienced pain all over my body. I also felt a lump in my throat as though I was choking. Sometimes I cried so much that the tears soaked the paper on which I was writing.

I can recall several reasons for my inability to share my grandmother's story. First of all, besides Mukaaka, no one else in the family talked about it. It was kept a secret. Although I felt pain, loss and a lack of an extended family typical of many African families, I dared not ask. My grandmother told me the story in secret and she preferred it to be kept this way. She often told it in the field or on our way to fetch water and firewood. She made sure we were alone, away from everyone else.

When I migrated to the United States of America, I thought to myself, "Surely, if I invite my mother to this country, she will feel comfortable enough to tell me what she knows about our family members who were lost in battle." I was wrong in making this assumption. When I attempted to talk to her about the subject, it caused her a lot of emotional distress. She did not want to talk about it. I insisted with the question, "Where did our people go?" Her quick response was: "Maybe some ended up in Buganda." This is the region of Uganda where the capital city, Kampala is located. I could tell from her response that she was just guessing and wanted to put an end to my questioning. From then on, I never attempted to bring up the subject again.

My precious mother passed away on December 23, 2010. Upon her departure, in the midst of grief, I heard a small voice inside me say: "You can tell your grandmother's story now. Her last-born child has just departed. You will not cause anyone pain. They are all at peace now. Telling the story will help heal your family and other families that have lost loved ones to senseless war and numerous other acts of violence."

Although I felt free to write this story at the end of the year 2010, it is now, almost nine years later, that I am finally gathering the courage to do so. Before giving up, I decided to seek God's help through intense prayer. I also got a lot of support from family members and friends who said to me, "This is a very important story. Please tell it."

Occasionally while on this journey, I asked myself, "Who is interested in the story of an African woman who lived in a village before the technological sophistications of television, the internet and cell phones?" I answered the question for myself thus: "You know that your grandmother can be called the "Wonder Woman of Burungu Village." She survived battle, raised her four children single-handedly and was an authority figure both in her home and community. She raised you, instilled in you wisdom, asked you to be an ambassador of peace and constantly reminded you to search for the people she lost. Many people from around the world would be interested in reading about her life."

I now have the stamina and strength to tell Mukaaka's story. This story is in no way auto-biographical. There is so much more about Mukaaka than these pages can contain. I am convinced that there is a lot more about her life than she was able to share with me. She knew that a mind of a child could carry limited information. She also selected to share with me those pieces of information that were most significant to her.

I am writing this story in the form of episodes that I experienced living with Mukaaka. I am also sharing those conversations that we had together. I also gathered a lot of information from her monologues, songs, prayers and proverbs. She was a very creative and effective communicator who used multiple approaches to sharing her message. Her photographic memory kept this story alive. Once in a while, she got her point across through dancing. She spoke Rutooro and I am translating what she said into English. I am sharing my testimony as someone who was raised by a battle-survivor and a peace-maker. Mukaaka gave me roots and wings.

The story in this book is real, not fictional. Mukaaka is a real person who lived in real time. I can feel her footsteps and hear her voice. My taste buds have tasted the food that she ate. Her story is rooted in the history of the Tooro people, Uganda, Africa and that of humanity the world over. I decided to search for historical evidence to support Mukaaka's story. Very key elders provided the much-needed information. I also consulted sources, both historical and current. The information that I received was priceless and helped me add evidence to the story. I am requesting my readers to get immersed in the context. Although I am writing in English, I am using expressions that are deeply-rooted in Tooro culture and Rutooro language that Mukaaka spoke.

I first approached writing this book almost as a reporter, a first witness to Mukaaka's life. I wanted to report the incredible experience I had growing up with a battle survivor and a widow. I wanted to talk about the life-giving skills that she passed on to me. Some of these include: faith in God, courage, hard work, humor, compassion, resourcefulness, self-discipline and many others.

The approach to this story from a reporter's perspective changed. I had to re-write the manuscript, using Mukaaka's own voice. I felt liberated because Mukaaka's voice can be heard, not mine. After reading the preface, you will encounter Mukaaka's voice in the succeeding chapters. My voice will return in the sections of Bidding Farewell, Setting the Context and the Epilogue.

When you read some words that are written in British English, do not be surprised. I first learned English in its British form. When you do see some American spelling and expression, please continue to enjoy reading the book. For the past thirty-seven years, I have lived, written, taught and raised my family in the United States of America. Through the years, I have adopted some American expressions and spelling.

In Mukaaka's story, I am also presenting the broader context, particularly political, religious and cultural that impacted our family. This book can also be viewed as a love letter from my grandmother to the world. Her testimony touches all people, world-wide. It also offers hope to all those people who daily experience tragedy and are survivors of catastrophes. It demonstrates the power of love, faith, community and the ability that lies in all of us to reach out and offer help to those in need. This book is a contribution to healing our world. Like any good medicine, it took a long time to come. Like any good medicine, its healing power runs deep.

Given the state of our world today which is filled with wars, violence and conflict, this book raises awareness of the harmful effects of these forces. It is also intended to encourage discussions regarding ways to curb war and violence. This book offers healing not just to my family but also to those other families all over the world that have lost loved ones through acts of violence. Hopefully, they too can gain the courage to tell their stories of loss and survival. Together, we can build a better and safer world for generations to come.

Through telling Mukaaka's story, I show the power of faith in molding a strong family that survived against all odds. The Church that spread the message of Jesus Christ was very instrumental in instilling the value of education and faith in Mukaaka's family. The last of her children, my mother received training as a teacher. She in turn passed on to me the love of education and the pursuance of excellence. I cherish these principles and strive daily to pass them on to my children and all the children of the world that I come in contact with either face-to-face or through my writing. I am saying: "No matter what happens, please hold on to God's unfailing love and always do your best to achieve your goals. When you fall, get up at once before you are trampled upon"

Unfortunately, I do not have any photographs of Mukaaka. I remember vaguely seeing a black and white photograph where she and I were together. My childhood photographs and other family memoirs got lost when our home crumbled to the ground. I lost additional photographs in my luggage on the way from Uganda to the United States in January of 1982. Fortunately, I have included a photograph of my mother that was taken in January of 2006. It is in the "Bidding Farewell" chapter. This is how Mukaaka looked during her eighties.

As you read this book, I am inviting you to befriend Mukaaka and draw inspiration from her. Several people have advised me to write my own life story. My quiet response has been, "Right now, the story that you need to read is Mukaaka's. She is the reason why there is a constant smile on my face and a sparkle in my eye. It is Mukaaka who taught me the value of always having the Joy that comes from God, how to build an extended family wherever I find myself and how to totally depend on God. She is the one who showed me, by her own acts of compassion, how to go beyond my own circumstances and help others who are in need."

Mukaaka befriended, fed, encouraged and was a positive influence to many. She never ignored or sent away the children that I brought home to be fed and to get help with their school assignments. She befriended the marginalized members of society and prayed for all of God's children to receive blessings. Her story teaches us all to respect and value the humanity of others, whether strangers or kin. In this book, the reader sees the power of God at work in places and people she/he has never met before.

It is an honour, privilege and a humbling experience to "pour out" this story that has been "sitting" deep within me for decades. As a new-born baby arrives and is held by loving hands, please hold Mukaaka's story with love and care. As you read this story, you will notice that I use Makaaka and Grandmother interchangeably.

Most of us have heard the popular African proverb which states: "It takes a village to raise a child." I would like to add to this ancient wisdom that it takes all of us to learn together, protect each other from harm, value those who came before us and to preserve the dignity of all humanity. I would also like you to connect this tragedy that took place in Africa with similar tragedies around the world both past and present. With this perspective in mind, we will refrain from repeating past mistakes that have caused harm to God's creation.

Read On.

JOURNEY OF NO RETURN

The girls in my family were considered a treasure because my mother produced six boys before the first girl arrived on the scene. She was given the special name of "Basemera" which is translated as; "They are Beautiful." The second girl was born four years after Basemera. She was named "Kabalinzi" which is translated as "Child of those who wait." I was born two years after Kabalinzi. My name was "Katusiime" which means "Let us be grateful." In addition to our given names, we also received praise names or "Empaako." Mine is Abwoli. My sister Kabalinzi was Akiiki and Basemera was Adyeri.

Empaako add charm, beauty and gentlesness to speech. The word "Empaako" comes from the verb "Kuhaaka" which means bestowing honor, praising, showing politeness or even a display of charm. It is also a way of displaying tact and applying proper negotiation skills. Empaako are used in greeting, saying "thank you" and saying "goodbye." Children are taught not to call their parents by their regular names. If ever they do, it is a sign of poor grooming, extreme disrespect or unruly behavior.

The benefits of using Empaako are many. They are

effective tools for instilling peace, love and community-building. Although these names had no meaning originally, with the passing of time, some of them have been associated with certain traits. Akiiki is called "Rukiikura Mahanga" which means "Savior or Helper of Nations." Apuuli is usually applied to little boys and Abwoli to little girls in instances where their names are not known. The elder does not feel obliged to find out what the young person's Empaako is. This is one of the benefits that come with age.

The people share eleven Empaako which include: Abbala, Abboki, Abwoli, Acaali, Adyeri, Akiiki, Amooti, Apuuli, Araali, Ateenyi and Atwoki. There is another one of these names that is reserved for the king. It is known as Okaali which is used during special ceremonies. For ordinary conversations, the king's Empaako is Amooti.

Basemera was endowed with big, beady, brown eyes. They are called "Amaiso g'ebituutu" and were admired by many. I had the best skin. It was very dark and smooth, known as "Omubiri gw'orubiindi.". The elders warned me never to bleach my skin with soaps and creams that were being sold in the markets. They were worried that some traditional beauty markers were starting to get lost. Kabalinzi's special feature was her dark, curly hair known as "ejwejwe." Village girls enjoyed braiding her hair because it did not easily break in their hands.

Kabalinzi also had a special feature in her mouth. Her upper front teeth had a gap in them known as "enana." These were planted on a very dark gum. Speaking of beauty, Kabalinzi had it. She was very well-endowed. The whole family knew she would not have trouble finding a suitor to marry her.

Before the invaders came to our village, life was normal. A regular day was full of happiness and productivity. Early in the morning, we were awakened by the birds that sang beautiful music into our ears. This, combined with the cock crow was the sign that it was time to get up and face the new day. We were taught to never oversleep. This behavior which is called "kuhetera" is for lazy people.

In all the homes, the mother or family matriarch was the first one to arise and to set a good example for everyone else. If the female of the home did not arise early, it was an indication that she was not feeling well. In our home, our mother always woke up before everyone else in the family. She said her morning prayers by lifting up her hands high to heaven. Sometimes she sang some songs.

Mother went straight to the kitchen, lit the fire and boiled water for the rest of the family to wash themselves. She then made breakfast which was usually millet porridge, roasted maize, cassava or sweet potatoes. Sometimes we ate warmed left-over food from the previous night. Because our family had cattle, drinking milk was part and parcel of the morning diet.

The children got out of bed right after our mother. It was one of the unbroken rules in our house that we all greeted each other in the morning. The children greeted the elders of the family while kneeling down and making sure that our eyes did not directly touch theirs. In our culture, if a child looks an elder in the eye, this is very impolite behavior.

Our father got up early too. He was a trader in the local market. Sometimes he rode his bicycle to several markets to buy and sell goods. On good days, after making sells of his goods that are called, "ekibambo," he brought home plenty of items. These included cow butter, ground nuts, salt, sugar, cooking oil and soap. Sometimes our father brought home some bread and a piece of cloth for our mother. He also bought clothes for us children.

After taking care of household duties, girls went with mother to the garden to cultivate crops. The boys took the animals for grazing. The afternoons offered us free time unless our home lacked firewood. In that case, the girls went deep into the woods to collect firewood.

In the evening, we joined our mother in preparing the evening meal. This often comprised of millet or mashed bananas called "omubumbo." Both of these are accompanied by sauce usually made out of beans, ground nuts or vegetables. Occasionally, we ate goat, beef, or chicken stew. When hunters returned from their hunting trips, they often brought us roasted buffalo meat. This made very delicious soup. One of my paternal uncles was a hunter. Our family received plenty of buffalo meat when he returned from hunting trips.

Afternoons were also times when the children had time off from our duties. This was the time when girls were allowed to braid each other's hair. We also played the game "Zaitumba" with other village girls. This game involved kicking stones. The boys usually spent many hours herding the animals. When they returned home, they played local football. This is what some people call soccer. They usually made their balls out of banana fibre.

Although we were not allowed to gossip or be involved in adult conversation, sometimes we did, hiding in the bushes. Some common topics included learning about the process of growing up, being involved with boys and having children. Those of us who were ten years of age and younger were not allowed by the older girls to join in these conversations. Since I had the reputation of being curious, I often hid behind a bush and overheard what the big girls were talking about.

One of the questions that the older girls asked each other was if they had started "being in the moon." Those who understood what being in the moon meant often giggled and responded in the affirmative. They talked about the monthly obligation and how this activity prepared them for motherhood.

I also heard from the girls that there were certain women in each family that were charged with the task of explaining to young girls the process of growing up, getting married and having children. These women were revered because they possessed great wisdom. They were often local midwives, shermans and spiritual healers. My aunt on my mother's side was one of these special women.

The evenings were usually filled with entertainment. After the evening meal, the women of the family gathered in the compound and educated the youth through songs, proverbs, riddles, and other forms of entertainment. The most popular type of music was called "enanga." Although I did not understand many of the messages when I was young, now that I am older, I do. These songs address a variety of subjects including beauty, love, romance, commitment and heartbreak. They also carry messages of good character and what a good spouse is like.

The men often sat in their own circles and taught young men how to be men. Common topics included principles of hard work, good character, good speech and how to be a good husband. On special days especially during harvest, men and women elders sat together to educate the children, celebrate success and also share pain. The drum was always present to share messages and provide music. Dancing the local, traditional dance known as "Orunyege" often accompanied the special occasions.

In many homes, locally-brewed beer called "amaarwa" was served. In my home, no alcohol was served. We served ensande, which is banana juice, water and porridge. Men who drank excessive alcohol were usually not well-regarded. They were called "Abatamiizi." Many ended up beating their wives, a behavior that is frowned upon.

I remember the good old days and often long for their return. Life was good before the strangers invaded our village. When they came and took away our people, they brought death with them. Those of us who survived are now here, trying to put together the pieces. I try to keep myself busy so that I can at least temporarily forget about the pain of losing my entire family. However much I try to forget, the question always remains: "Where did my people go?"

That fateful morning, everything started off very peacefully. Dew was still on the grass and the sun's rays were shining bright. The birds were singing their cheerful melodies. None of us suspected that this day would be the last for us to be with our family. We had no idea that going to the well to fetch water would lead to the journey of no return.

In our family, all of us knew our duties. The girls fetched water and firewood while the boys looked after cows and goats. We left for the well that morning, while the boys were still at home. They were cleaning the animal and chicken sheds. Mother was peparing millet porridge for breakfast. Father was getting ready to go to the local market to sell hides and skins.

When we heard the gun shots, they sounded like many calabashes, "ebisisi," being broken all at the same time. Sometimes this sound was mixed with one that was like thunderstorms. We started to hear people wailing. The animals and chickens were all screaming and restless.

In our predicament, we huddled around each other, shaking with fear. As we stood there, stiff, cold and trembling, our oldest sister, Basemera, whispered: "Those must be the strangers that the chief warned us about. They have invaded our home. We can't go back home now. We must run and hide."

Basemera advised us to run and hide in the bushes. She also told us to take our water pots with us in order to avoid being traced and found. With tears streaming out of our eyes, the three of us went into hiding. Basemera was twelve years of age. Yes, she was about that age with tiny fruits beginning to appear on her chest. Kakwanzi was eight and I was six years old.

Before the sad day when starangers came to our home and took my entire family, the chief had warned us of impending doom. He talked about strangers who were kidnapping people and taking them away. He had received these messages from the king. The fearless and ruthless strangers comprised of neighboring King Kabalega's army known of "Abarusura." They had sophisticated weapons that killed instantly. Some of these weapons had smoke that came out of their mouths. They were nick-named "Kanwa Kabi" meaning "Bad Mouth." When the poison from their mouths got in touch with any living thing, there was instant death. The chief told the people to travel around in groups. This was particularly essential while travelling at night.

Although people lived in fear because of the impending doom, they went about performing their duties. They cultivated the land, planted and harvested crops. They also looked after their livestock and provided for the young. Weddings were performed and babies were born. Many children were given names with the theme of war. Girls were named "Kabarwaani" meaning "Child of Fighters" while boys were named "Murwaani" which means "Fighter."

The chief's words were confirmed through dreams and visions that the local prophets and prophetesses were experiencing. Several of them mentioned strange smoke that was filling the air. Others talked about famine, death and utter hopelessness that were coming in large quantities. They advised people of all ages to take these words seriously. One particular prophetess spoke of a time when grain stores "enguli" would be turned upside down and when houses would be inhabited by spiders, rats, snakes and frogs because their rightful owners would be gone.

As we crept under the bushes, drenched in morning dew, we all remembered the days that had been foretold. Our little dresses got wet and stuck to our small bodies. While looking for a hiding place in the forest, we tried to avoid getting too close to the river. We had been warned by the elders to be careful while crossing this river. Although it was not very big, it had sinkholes in some areas that caused people to drown.

We hid under a big, tall tree with branches that spread in every direction. A sad incident took place under this tree. As we lay there, a large, black snake came down from one of the branches. It bit my second oldest sister, Kabalinzi. Basemera and I lay there, motionless, pretending to be dead. The snake climbed back to the top of the tree. After the snake bite, Basemera and I made some movements. Kabalinzi lay there still and lifeless. Basemera shook her body in an attempt to wake her up. Her efforts were in vain. The snake's poison had taken our dear sister's life.

These types of snakes, called "enchweera" are well-known for their extremely poisonous venom. Some village elders who were local herbalists had medicine to treat people who had snake bites. Sadly, Kabalinzi was not lucky to receive the treatment. We were away from home, gone on a journey of no return.

Upon realizing that Kabalinzi was gone, the two of us sobbed without making noise. We dug a small grave using sharp sticks and our hands. We then placed our sister's lifeless body in it, gathered leaves, tree branches and soil and covered her. With sorrow mixed with pain and fear, we said "good-bye" to our beautiful sister and left. The two of us walked close to one another in the opposite direction from our home. We crossed the river at a shallow spot where we could not drown. After crossing the river, we sat down in an area with tall grass. The morning sunshine warmed our bodies and the heat dried our dresses.

After getting warm, Basemera and I started walking again. We came across a field of sweet potatoes and maize. Basemera advised me to go into the field to get some food. At first, I hesitated because our parents had taught us that it was wrong to steal from others. Upon noticing my hesitation, Basemera told me that this was not stealing. God was giving us food for the journey. She added that if the owner showed up, we would tell him/her our story and hopefully we would receive mercy. Upon hearing these words from my sister, I followed her advice. We got some potatoes and maize, wrapped them in grass and continued on our journey. Each one of us carried "entanda" meaning "packed lunch."

We continued walking, crossed a grassy area, and passed through a banana plantation. We got some banana leaves and wrapped our food very securely. After walking for about two miles, we came to a small, grass house known as, "ekisu." There was a blind, old lady sitting outside the house, warming up in the morning sun. She was humming to herself a beautiful traditional song, "Ngayaya." I had often heard my maternal grandmother sing this beautiful music.

We greeted the old lady very politely, using her title "Omukaikuru" meaning "Respectable Old Lady." She also told us her empaako of Atwoki. This made our communication easy. We told her our story and wailed out loud at the mention of our sister Kabalinzi's name. The old lady was very sympathetic towards us. She told us that her village had also been warned about the invaders. She added that some of her village members were making plans to leave.

We instantly felt at home with the old lady. She reminded us of our own grandmothers and other elders in our village. She also acted towards us as our real grandmother would. When we spoke to her, we bent a little, avoiding standing there in front of her as though we were trees. We also made sure our eyes did not directly look into hers.

Our newly-found grandmother shared with us her decision to stay and die in her home. Her husband had passed away the year before and she saw no reason for leaving. When we told her that we had raw sweet potatoes and maize, she let us go inside the house to roast them in the fireplace. She also directed us to go to the corner of the house and get small gourds, "enkooba" in which to carry water. She told us to fill our gourds with water from the clay pot, "ensoha" that sat in the opposite corner of the house. We were very grateful and thanked her by saying: "Webale muno Atwoki." This means, "Thank you very much Atwoki."

We spent more time chatting with our elder. She told us that she had been blinded by a disease called "Oburundu" which means "Smallpox." Her parents gave her the formula for making the powder to cure snake bites. Every time a snake bit her, she dissolved her powder in water and drank it, thereby receiving instant healing.

Our new friend had grandchildren who lived close by and took care of her. They filled her pot with water, cleaned her house and prepared her meals. Every morning, one of them came to take her outside to be in the sun and returned later to bring her back into the house. She often wondered what would happen to her when all her children decided to run away from the invaders.

Before setting off on our journey, Grandmother Atwoki advised us to stay with her for at least ten more days so that we could complete the ceremony called "Kuturuka Orufu" which means "Coming out of death." She told us that after going through the ceremony, we would at least come to terms with the death of our beloved sister. The ceremony also helps the soul of the departed to rest in peace.

Upon hearing our new grandmother's advice, we thanked her and made the decision to stay with her family for at least ten more days. Basemera reminded me of a similar ceremony that we had in our family when our paternal grandfather passed away the previous year. Because he was an elder in the family, the ceremony lasted an entire week. Among other activities that we had to go through, our hair was shaved off our heads.

As the sun began to set, two of Grandmother Atwoki's grandchildren came to take her back into the house. She introduced us to them and shared our story. We could tell they were twin girls because their names were Nyangoma and Nyakato. Twins are treated in a very special way in our culture. They even receive special names. An instant bonding took place between us. Upon hearing about Kabalinzi's death, they started crying and offered us comfort.

Later on that evening, Grandmother Atwoki's daughter came to see her. Makune was her name. This name can simply be translated as "Hospitality or Generosity." Makune brought with her a delicious meal of millet, green vegetables and mashed beans called "Firinda." Her husband "Baguma" which means, "They are Strong", also stopped by on his way from work. Upon hearing our sad story, the couple offered us comfort and invited us to dinner. For a brief moment, my siter Basemera and I felt as though we were in our own home.

Atwoki and her family organized the ceremony to officially say "goodbye" to our sister. The entire village was invited and people brought a lot of food. We prayed, sang songs and the elders told stories about the Batooro people. We met many people who were our relatives through the clan system.

A small grave was dug in honor of our sister. We in turn threw in soil and planted in a tree called "Akayenje," as a symbol of her life. Grandmother Atwoki told us that we could shave our hair in honor of our sister, as a sign of love and respect. It is also a way of showing an unbreakable bond. She also added that since she left as a child, we could keep our hair. Removing just a little bit would be enough. We decided to remove just a little bit and kept the rest of our hair.

After staying with Grandmother Atwoki and her family a few more days, we left for our journey. Generous people gave us a lot of food, drink and pieces of cloth to sustain us on the journey. The day of our departure was a very sad one. Many people came to say goodbye to us. The elders advised us not to cry because tears would bring bad luck to us. Instead, we were showered with plenty of prayers, hugs and blessings.

We said goodbye to the kind lady and the entire community that had embraced us. We walked many miles and were joined by other people who were trying to run away from the captors.

Banana Plantation

GRANDMOTHER'S STORY

Lake Wabikere   *Lake Saka*

On the long journey, we crossed banana plantations, passed by crater lakes, climbed hills and kept on walking.

Some strong people in the group who did not have babies of their own carried other people's babies on their backs. I was one of those children who drew a lot of sympathy from the crowd. Many strong people often carried me and made the journey a little lighter. When our food supply ran out, we ate roots, leaves, berries and other fruits

Many people were worried about crossing River Kanywankoko. Its name can be translated as "The One Who Drinks Chickens." Many living things, including humans often drowned in this river. Stories were told that this river was also home to crocodiles, snakes and many other creatures. Often, some of them climbed up to the river banks. The possibility of coming face-to-face with one or more of these creatures frightened many people who crossed this river.

Although River Kanywankoko looks old and sluggish now, it was once very powerful. It roared and frightened many living creatures, including humans. It showed great fury and appeared to be boiling its own water in anger.

Kambuzi Hill *Kyatwa Hill*

Legend had it that this river had taken so many lives that their spirits occasionally rose up, demanding their lives back. They beat their drums from the bottom of the river. This calmed down the mighty river, at least temporarily. People often heard these drums and nick-named the river, "Ngomaigamba" which means "Drums Talk."

River Kanywankoko had no bridge. There were two poles that lay across, side by side. The people who had good balance crossed it very easily. However, many others lost their balance and drowned. People were warned not to drink any alcohol before crossing this river. Those who disobeyed the warning and attempted to cross the river in an intoxicated state often lost their balance and drowned.

After walking for a very long distance, we reached River Kanywankoko. I remember my sister and I simply standing at the edge of the river, too afraid to cross it. Down below, we could see the water fuming as though ready to swallow someone. When my eyes saw the water,

River Kanywankoko

I felt as though life was leaving my tiny body. I fell to the ground and could not see anything around me. My sight was completely gone. In my predicament, I heard a deep male voice ask, "Onu omwaana abaire ki?" which means, "What is wrong with this child?"

As I lay there wondering what to do, at once, I felt strong, large hands lift me up and sweep me off the ground. I felt like a small chick in its mother's mouth, being led to safety. In a few minutes, I found myself on the other side of the river, with the rest of the group. My sight had fully returned to me. I could not tell whether the hands that carried me across the river were those of a living person, a departed ancestor or an angel sent to me by God.

Fear departed from me as I looked around to thank the person who had carried me across the river. Unfortunately, most of the people had moved on. I also started looking for my sister Basemera. I had no doubt that she too would be looking for me. "Surely, she did not move on, leaving her little sister behind," I said to myself.

Many of the people who crossed River Kyanywankoko remained on their journey. They continued walking on to find an escape. Although I have no idea where their journey took them, they left some of us at the edge of the river. I will never know who helped me cross the big river. I still feel the grip of the large hands. This was a mighty grip that carried me through. I was carried over to safety. Since I was safe, my hope increased. I had no doubt that more help for me was on the way.

After searching for my sister in vain, I sat down among the people who had decided to stay at the edge of River Kanywankoko. Many of these were too tired to move on. Most of them were children, the elderly and expectant mothers. The majority of them had simply lost hope and decided to die at this place.

The left-behind group decided to move away from the banks of River Kanywankoko. We walked and sat at the edge of a calm crater lake whose name is Balamu, meaning, "They are Alive."

We camped at Lake Balamu, awaiting our fate. We became an instant family. Occasionally, someone caught some fish from the lake that gave us food. At night, we huddled around each other. I covered myself with the cloth, "Esuuka" that Grandmother Atwoki had given to me. I hoped and prayed that God would help us and that somehow I would be reunited with my sister Basemera.

Several expectant mothers gave birth to babies at Lake

Balamu. Whenever a mother went into labor, the women surrounded her and took her to a nearby bush. They covered her with their pieces of cloth, making her as comfortable

Lake Balamu

as possible. Someone, usually a man or elderly lady shouted, "Pray. A baby is being born." There was no shortage of midwives. Hope returned through the bith of a new baby whose introduction came with a loud cry. Each time, the whole group agreed on the name for the baby.

As I continued to search for my sister, I saw men approaching us. They looked like us and shouted, "mutatiina" which means, "don't fear." They were carrying weapons and wore heavy, noisy boots. They announced that they were soldiers of the king. They had been sent to take the survivors to the palace. We climbed on the lorry that was parked a short distance from the lake. The elderly were helped to climb on the lorry first. These were followed by expectant mothers and small children. The stronger, younger men and women entered last. I do not remember anything regarding the trip from the river to the palace. I was asleep all the way.

LIFE AT KARUZIIKA

I woke up just in time to see the grand entrance to Karuziika the Palace. At first, I thought this was a mere dream. Within a short time, it was real. I had just arrived at a place where the king lived. Instantly, fear departed from me and I felt surrounded by peace. I sighed with relief and said to myself: "ehu." I had heard this word uttered many times before in my birth home. When there was a major accomplishment such as giving birth, women said "ehu." After bringing home water, firewood or food, whoever had accomplished the task said "ehu." This word is an expression of total relief, the equivalent of "finally."

There were tall, strong men who helped us get off the lorry. I looked around me and saw the beautiful palace that was surrounded by several houses. Those of us who had just arrived were led to houses that from then on, we would call home. Males and females were led to different houses. Seven young girls, including myself were led to a house called Kabagarama. The ladies that led us to our home told us that we were called "banyaanya" or sisters of the king. All of us who stayed at this house were less than ten years of age.

The ladies who led us to our house were dressed in white uniforms like those of nurses. They spoke to us very kindly and welcomed us to our new home. After showing us our beds, they left us in the house and returned with food. After eating, we were led to a place where we cleaned ourselves before going to bed. Two of the white-uniformed ladies spent the night at our house.

Early in the morning, the two ladies woke us up and told us that they were our caretakers. They fed us and gave us new clothes. They told us that Batebe, the king's sister was coming to welcome us. We were under her guardianship. Batebe came into our house and gave us a very warm welcome. She told us that we had been adopted into this family and that we were princesses from henceforth.

Even though we belonged to different clans, we were adopted by the Babiito, the ruling clan. She said that we were going to learn the language and culture of the palace. After meeting her, we were led to greet the king. The proper greeting of the king is "Zoona Okaali', while kneeling down. This greeting is an expression of absolute respect, honor and surrender. Even old people kneel to greet the king, which is a big honor.

Life at Karuziika was very interesting. We followed a daily routine that kept us healthy and well-informed. Our routine consisted of getting up early in the morning. After getting clean and dressed, we gathered for morning prayer and ate breakfast. After that, we went to greet the king. Greeting the king is called "Kuramya."

We were taught the language, etiquette and culture of

the palace, learned everyday subjects including numbers and science. We were also taught arts and crafts, history, especially of our kingdom, hygiene, food preparation, cleaning and farming. We also had drills in which we learned how to exercise and had religious education.

There was also a lot of entertainment at Karuziika. The times I enjoyed most were during the dance called Amakondere and the celebration of Empango. I also looked forward to attending church services and weddings. During these special occasions, we wore very clean and beautiful clothes.

Women and Children of the Palace

King Kyebambe got baptized into the Christian faith in 1896 and was given the name Daudi that means David. He took his faith very seriously. He was determined to "remove darkness and usher in light" (Oyo@18). Growing up at the palace, we all practiced the Christian faith.

My baptism name in the Protestant church was Luz. I also received a new tribal name called Kabahenda. I learned later on that the army of King Kaboyo Olimi I, the first king of Tooro was named "Abahenda" (Oyo@18). I must have been named after that army, my name literally meaning, " Child of the Abahenda Army." My baptism name remained Luz until after getting married and joining my husband's faith in the Catholic church. The nuns slightly changed my name to Rwiiza.

King Kyebambe was a very kind and compassionate person. He was always very proud of his family that included us, the battle orphans that he had adopted. This king was also very well-educated, having had his schooling at the highly-reputed King's College, Budo.

Young Kyebambe at Budo College

His love for education, emphasis on positive change and equality between men and women led him to the founding of Kyebambe Girls School that still exists today.

Kyebambe Girls School

Kyebambe Girls School

At Karuziika, I got to meet many important people, including members of royalty from other kingdoms. I also met diplomats from other nations. I remember a time in

1906 when King Kyebambe received the Duke from Italy. All of us lined up to greet these special visitors.

Visitors at the Palace

Visitors at the Palace

During my stay at the palace, I continued looking for my sister Basemera. As more children were brought in, my hope was that she would be among them. With the passing of time, my hope evaporated. I came to learn that many people had continued running. They either disappeared in the mountains, drowned in rivers and lakes or were captured by the invaders. Others became pray to wild animals. Up to now, I have no answer regarding Basemera's or my entire family's whereabouts. Whenever I feel as though a sharp knife is piercing my chest, I pray to God and ask the question, "Where did my people go?"

During my teenage years, I caught the attention of several young men who wanted to marry me. They admired me for my beauty, good character and work habits. They also liked the fact that I took my Christian faith very seriously. I was serious but very pleasant to be around. I admired young men only from a distance. Several proposed to me but I refused their offer to marry me. I did not want to disappoint my family by being pre-maturely involved with men. I wanted to wait for the right one.

The right man for me came when I was about nineteen years old. His name was Kachope. He was one of King Kyebambe's attendants. Whenever he saw me outside carrying out my daily duties, I could tell that I drew his attention. I could almost hear his heart beat faster than normal. Instead of proposing to me directly, a middle man called "Kibonabuko" was sent to the king with a proposal to marry me. This process is known as "Kweranga."

King Kyebambe discussed the matter with the Queen and Batebe. There were no long negotiations since there was no bridewealth required. In case of princesses, the groom brings no bridewealth. Instead, the king showers the bride with gifts to start her off in her marriage. The three agreed that Batebe should break the news to me, which she did. Without displaying "greed" for men, I first refused. Kachope's relentlessness proved that he was the right man for me.

Kachope had to pass a test in order to prove that I was the one that he had selected among many girls. A day was chosen for him to come and select his bride. He returned with Kibonabuko and several members of his family. During this process, the groom relies on the elders to speak on his behalf. This is to avoid any mistake whatsoever. Many girls, ranging in age from very young to old ladies were lined up for Kachope to select his bride. He politely said "No" every time I was not included in the group. Finally, time came for me to come out with another group.

Kachope was very happy and excited to select his bride. I was also overcome with exteme joy. When the Elder asked me the question: "Is this the right man you are bringing to us?", I said: "Yes." All those who were present clapped their hands and a big feast followed.

A period of courtship called "Kujumbirwa" followed. Our courtship lasted a whole year. During this period, I was full of anxiety that was mixed with joy. I was glad that I was going to spend my entire life with someone who had loved me and chosen me from among many other girls. I was anxious to enter into marriage and to have children of my own.

During many nights, I thought about Kachope and our new home. He looked kind and I trusted that he would treat me well. I was confident that he would always remember that I was the king's sister, a princess that should be held as someone precious and breakable known as "Ekirukwatika." Although I was anxious about my new life, God was the source of my comfort. I had no doubt that Kachope would be a good husband to me and a wonderful father to our children.

According to tradition, a bride-to-be does not walk around for days, weeks or even months before the wedding. She stays in a special room where attendants meet her needs. She is fed very well and speaks very softly. Every day, her entire body is covered with special oil to keep it smooth, beautiful and soft.

While in this special room, elderly ladies came to pay me visits. They shared with me their secrets of how to have a happy and successful marriage. I enjoyed the visits from these special ladies. Sometimes each one came alone and occasionally they came as a group.

During this special time, the ladies opened up and relived their courtship experiences with great affection and nostalgia. They sang to me the special songs called "enanga." They carefully selected the songs that expressed the themes of love and romance. I was very surprised to see these ladies in a playful mood. I was used to seeing them looking strict and serious in public.

For an entire year, I went through the process of learning how to be a good wife. Kachope proposed to me in 1906 and we got married in 1907. I remember we got married one year after the Italian Duke visited our kingdom. We had a grass-thatched palace then. King Kyebambe built a more modern one thereafter.

During my period of courtship, I did not walk alone. When I needed to go out and walk in the sun, I went with an escort. Besides avoiding strain on my skin resulting from too much exposure to the sun, I had to keep myself safe. Since Kachope had given me orukwanzi, (long, white necklace of beads), I had to remain protected from the eyes of other men. I was even kept away from Kachope to avoid any temptation whatsoever. Those were the good old days when love was pure, simple and uncomplicated.

I had two weddings, a traditional and a church one. The traditional wedding ceremony took place on Friday evening, the day before the church wedding. If Iwas not a Christian, this customary wedding would have been enough. During the traditional wedding ceremony, I was dressed in Orubugo, which is the bark cloth. My aunts sat in a circle and I took turns sitting on their laps. This was after they gave me additional instructions about married life. Kachope was also given instructions by the uncles. We exchanged our vows before the king, the royal family and special invited guests.

Following the vows, Kachope placed another necklace around my neck. It was a mixture of white and gold. In return, I placed a special hat on his head. The marriage was sealed. In the evening, before the big feast, King Kyebambe showered me with many gifts that included cattle, expensive jewelry and cloth.

We had our church wedding on Saturday, following the traditional wedding. Early in the morning, the ladies attending to me woke me up and gave me a bath. After taking a bath , I had breakfast with the other Banyaanya that occupied the Kabagarama house. My beautiful white wedding dress hang in my room. After breakfast, the Banyaanya left so that they could start getting ready for the big day. I remained in my room where the ladies made sure my nails were cut and my hair was well-done.

On this special morning, Batebe came early to my room to say farewell to me. When the time came for me to go and greet the King, she embraced me and cried. We were very close to each other. She told me that she was going to miss me. I also shed some tears.

When the princess left the room, the other Banyaanya took turns to come and bid me farewell. They each gave me a gift to accompany me on the journey. For the whole year when I was in the large room, my sisters made gifts for me. These gifts included jewelry, baskets, mats and dresses. Some even made handbags for me.

At around eleven o'clock in the morning, my attendees and I went to greet the king who was seated in his special chair. I was wearing orubugo, my traditional cloth. My neck, wrists and ankles were adorned with special jewelry. My hair was decorated with very elegant beads of many colors.

I knelt before the King and he touched my shoulders to bless me. I felt very grateful to this great person who had given me a chance at life. At that point, I began to sob endlessly. He held my hands for quite some time and handed my hands over to my chief escort. I felt as though a river of fresh water was flowing through my entire body.

Before going back to my room, I sat on the King and Queen's laps to receive the final blessing. When I returned to the room, my helpers got me dressed in my white dress. I had white matching shoes and a white handbag to hold. At exactly one o'clock in the afternoon, I walked to the hall for the wedding ceremony. I was escorted by my seven sisters who wore pink dresses. Everywhere, I passed, there were flowers on the floor.

We walked slowly, got to the hall and found Kachope waiting for me. He had his own escorts of young, handsome gentlemen with him. When I laid my eyes on my husband-to-be, my heart jumped in my chest. Here was a dark, tall, handsome man that was going to be mine forever. He held a stick called "omwiigo" that was decorated with beads.

As a sign of politeness, I made sure my eyes and Kachope's did not directly meet. I held back tears because I wanted to be brave. King Kyebambe, Batebe and the whole family were there for me. Kachope and I got married at the large hall in the palace. Since both of us were baptized in the Christian church, there was a Christian Minister called "Omwahule" to conduct the wedding ceremony.

The wedding ceremony was followed by a party that was attended by many people. We received more gifts from members of the family and friends. The hall was full to the brim. Some people sat on the verandah and in the palace courtyard. At around 5 o'clock in the evening, a large crowd escorted us to the special car that the King had set aside to take us to Kinyamasika to our new home. One of the escorts held a black umbrella over our heads. A black umbrella at a wedding is a symbol of wealth, prosperity and good luck. Throughout the entire wedding process, coffee beans were served.

A driver appointed by the king drove us from the palace to our new home. He drove the well-decorated large vehicle very slowly. Wherever we passed, people waved at us. Several other cars carrying my sisters and the many gifts that I had received followed us.

When we arrived at my new husband's home, many people were waiting for us. Drummers, singers and dancers were all performing. The dancers were dancing "orunyege," a popular dance in the village. My escorts were with me. The first activity for me was to sit on the laps of my father-in- law and mother-in- law. In our tradition, this is a sign of being born into one's family of marriage. For a blessing, I was sprinkled with herbal water called "endemezi."

We were directed to a large room where we were fed delicious food. My entire group went back home that evening. The only person who remained with me was a little girl called Kemigisa. I called her my little sister. Kachope and I stayed together in this room for one week. Special attendants were selected to take care of our needs. Since I had not "known" a man before my wedding, my family received special honor. Ordinarily, my parents would have received heads of cattle and plenty of other gifts. Since I was a princess, my father the King sent my husband and I more precious gifts.

On the seventh day after the wedding, some members of my family came back to my new home and we had a ceremony called "kuruga ha rusiika." During this celebration, my party led me out of the room and accompanied me outside. We sat in a tent called "ekijaraja." The people on my husband's side of the family were able to look at me and shower me with praises through songs. My husband and I received more gifts from his side of the family. This was also the day when I prepared my first meal of millet. The festivities of the day went on till the evening hours. After that, my party left for home. Since that day, our marriage was off to a good start.

FROM THE PALACE TO THE VILLAGE

After moving to Kinyamasika village, my husband and I built our own house, sharing the same compound with his large family of the Bayaga clan. His parents lived in the center of the compound. Houses of the three brothers, their wives and children surrounded the parents' house. His three older sisters were already married and lived in other villages.

We started off our marriage very well. The wedding gifts offered us a good start. Besides cattle, we had many household items that were not found in an average home. I also brought with me a basket full of jewelry known as "Ekiibo ky'enkwanzi." I gave some of these away to my in-laws and friends of the family.

Our house was a few yards outside the family circle. I wanted my own privacy but hardly got any. The family extended way beyond our compound to include other relatives and almost the entire village. People wanted to know everything about me. They often called me "Omuhumakati wa ha Kikaali" meaning "The Royal One from the Palace."

Although I did not want to stand out in my husband's

village, I did. People wanted to hear me talk. They also wanted to see if I could cook, wash, clean and do farm work. Mind you, I had just come from the place where we had helpers to do the "sweat work." Even though I had been instructed on how to perform duties of married life, they were too difficult for me to handle.

When I went to do the back-breaking farm work, I often got very tired. I was not used to bending my back for so long. I was humiliated by the fact that the wives of my husband's brothers knew how to till the ground, plant crops, do the weeding and harvest the crops. They often tied their youngest babies on their backs and left for the fields very early in the morning. One of them was nicknamed a tractor. The tractor was this large machine that looked like a lorry. It came from Bungereza (Europe) or America. I wished my husband Kachope had one of those tractors to help us.

I often wanted to go back to the palace. I even wished I could meet my sister Basemera somewhere in the village so that she might help me with the work and keep me company. During many nights, I cried, wanting to be with my families, the one at the palace and the one into which I was born.

In my sad moments, I remembered some of the stories that my grandmother told me when I was little. Maybe she knew that we were going to be torn apart as a family by tragedy. My grandmother, who had beautiful, gray hair told me that grandmothers never leave their favorite little girls. After death, they always return in the spirit form to help their loved ones.

GRANDMOTHER'S STORY

I recalled two stories which my grandmother told me about the return of the ancestors. Both stories involved ancestors who returned to assist their loved ones and led them to success. The first story was about a young bride whose mother had passed away without teaching her daughter how to till the land. Her husband and the whole family called her lazy and despised her.

The young bride often went to bed hungry and cried herself to sleep. In her desperation, she talked to her mother through a song. One day when she was working in the fields, her mother returned. She got the hoe from her daughter and demonstrated to her the right way to cultivate the land. She repeated this activity several times until her daughter learned the lesson. After that, she left and never came back.

The second story that conveyed the same meaning of an ancestor returning to help a suffering relative involved a little bird. The bird was sent as an ambassador from a deceased grandmother to help her granddaughter. The young lady had faced a lot of misfortune. First of all, she was barren. Because she bore no children, her husband's family mistreated her. They made arrangements for him to marry another wife from the neighboring village. They gave the new wife the name "Kiganzi" which means "The Loved One."

As soon as the second wife arrived, life became unbearable for the first wife. The family gave her the name "Kinobi" which means "The Disliked One." She was also referred to as the "Woman With Bad Fortune." Despite

37

her charm, beauty and a generous spirit, the whole family turned against her. She lived in her house alone and suffered in silence. Her husband built a large, beautiful house for the new wife where he spent most of his time.

On several occasions, Kinobi attempted to run away. She was not successful. Her parents had died and there was no way she could return the bride wealth that her husband had given before he married her. In those days, it was not uncommon for a beautiful bride's family to receive many heads of cattle, cloth and expensive jewelry.

During her sad days, Kinobi shared her problems with close friends. They tried to offer her comfort the best way they could. Unfortunately, they were unable to help her bear a child. They were also unable to turn her land into a productive field just like that of the second wife. The soil was poor and full of rocks. Because it was located on a hillside, whenever heavy rain fell, it washed away the good soil, leaving behind hard, rocky soil.

In her desperation, Kinobi cried out to her grandmother for help. She had heard from village elders that when people die, they do not depart completely. Death is merely a change of address. She learned that upon death, the spirit leaves the body and lives on. This lesson never departed from her. She held onto it as a baby clings to the mother's chest.

One day when Kinobi was tilling her hard ground, a little bird called "Enyonza" stopped by and started singing. This family of birds is well-known for their gentle, soothing music. Early in the morning, they often wake up people to face the new day. These birds play the role of modern-day alarm clocks. They are also known as birds that carry good fortune. While some birds carry bad news such as announcing war or death, Enyonza announce health, peace, and wealth.

At first, Kinobi did not pay much attention to the little bird's singing. She thought to herself, "What fortune can you bring to me at this time in my life? Can you remove Kiganzi from her throne? Can you help me bear children? Can you make this hard rocky soil productive?" As a matter of fact, instead of soothing her, the music from the little bird made Kinobi irritated and upset. She even thought of chasing the little bird away.

Instead of driving the little bird away, Kinobi decided to take a break from her hard labor. She sat down under a tree and started eating her packed lunch while looking up at the noonday sun. In a loud voice, she called; "Grandmother, come and help me. Because I am lonely, with no company, I am now eating with birds. Why haven't you returned to help me? Have you forgotten about your little girl with a gap in her teeth?"

While still pleading for her grandmother's return, Kinobi heard the following words come from the bird seated on the tree branch above her head; "I am an ambassador from your grandmother. I have been sent to comfort you. I am now leaving and going to confuse your husband's new wife. I will go there, flatter her and make her grow a big head. She will put her hoe aside and get full of herself.

In the end, her land will not produce. I will then return to your land and build ridges around these slopes. The ridges will stop soil from being washed away by the rain. I will also invite the birds from my family to come and help you. We will bring fertilizer to make your land productive."

The following day, the bird that had visited Kinobi went to Kiganzi's field. With the help of paid servants, Kiganzi was tilling her land. The bird sat in a tree nearby and started singing flattering words. The words went like this:

"The bird from far away has come to tell you that you are a great farmer. Your co-wife Kinobi is useless and lazy. You are doing a very good job. See how you are turning the soil inside-out? You are the best. I am not lying."

Upon hearing these words, Kiganzi and her helpers became filled with pride. They stopped working and started partying in the field. Kiganzi brought drink and food with her to the field every day. Instead of working, her helpers started being obnoxious. They lost respect for their boss. Kiganzi took to drinking alcohol. The men elevated themselves to being her lovers while the women servants became disrespectful and rude.

Kiganzi, the woman who was the family's favorite fell from grace and embarrassed herself. Her parents and two sons also got embarrassed. Instead of experiencing peace in the home, violence erupted between Kiganzi and her husband. While Kiganzi was going downhill, Kinobi started recovering from her unfortunate ordeal.

The little bird brought her relatives who helped Kinobi till the land. She planted crops that yielded plenty of food. The new friends even introduced her to a local doc-

GRANDMOTHER'S STORY

tor who gave her medicine to cure her infertility. In five years, Kinobi bore seven children who included three sets of twins. Her four daughters and three sons comforted her and helped her in the fields.

Before long, Kinobi, the wife who was doomed to fail, was restored to her rightful position. The new wife went back to her parents. She left her two sons with their father. Her whole extended family was humiliated. Her parents had to return the bride wealth. As for Kinobi, her good fortune was multiplied. Kinobi and her children moved into the big house where her husband lived. She was given all the land. She and her children became the rightful heirs to the family's wealth. Her name Kinobi was changed overnight to "Kamaani" which means "Full of Strength."

All the village members heard about the young woman who had received favor from her deceased grandmother. The news was spread to other villages. On market days, the story was told and it spread like wildfire. Even musicians composed songs about the wonderful, powerful ancestors who help their living relatives to solve their problems.

Grandmother's stories comforted me. Instead of feeling afraid most of the time, I gained confidence. I was sure my brave and loving ancestors would one day come to my rescue. I also found a lot of comfort in the church. After getting married, I had converted to Catholicism, the religion of my husband and his family. I became very close to the nuns. I also found a lot of comfort in the Virgin Mary, the mother of Jesus. I believed that she had adopted me as her own child. Whenever I said the Rosary, I felt very close to her.

My husband and I had three children during the first six years of our marriage. They came "running," following each other, two years apart. We named our first-born daughter "Kabachanda" which means "Child of the Suffering." She also received Empaako of "Akiiki." At baptism, she was named Catherine which is locally called, "Katalina."

Our second daughter was named "Kabadaaki." She was born during the time when Dutch people visited our country. We gave her the Empaako "Amooti" and she received a baptism name of Helen which is locally called "Herena."

A boy followed the two girls. We named him "Tinkasimire," which means "I am not yet grateful." He received the Empaako "Apuuli" and Archaengel was the name given to him at baptism. In the village, he was known as "Erikanjeru."

As time went by, village life became easier. I often dreamed of my grandmother coming to my home to help me especially to grind millet and to help me with work in the fields. The family and other villagers got to know me better and opened up to me. Many were very sympathetic when I shared with them how I had lost my entire family.

Kachope was a kind and loving man. He often hired workers to help me in the fields and with housework. He was very faithful and promised me that he would never marry more wives like some other men did. He believed

GRANDMOTHER'S STORY

that when people get married, they should remain faithful to each other. He often said that love cannot be divided up among several partners.

My husband did not drink alcohol. This was a big surprise to many men. He came home early and took care of me and the children. He often took me with him to the market to help him count money from his sales. Some jealous women went around gossiping that I carried my husband as though he was my hand bag. Kachope often told me to ignore them.

Kachope was a trader in hides and skins just like my own biological father. He bought his merchandise from neighboring Congo. He often went on trading trips that lasted several months. Many people teased me by saying that in Kachope, I saw my own father. They said that some girls look for husbands who are like their own father.

I never disputed the fact that Kachope reminded me of my father. Many men came asking for my hand in marriage. I turned them down until Kachope showed up. These are things that are hard for me to explain. What I know is that he was handsome, well-mannered and persistent in getting me. When others gave up at the first "no", he kept coming until the tenth time when I finally said "yes."

We were a model family, upright in character. We trained our children to be polite and hard-working. King Kyebambe constantly asked about me and advised my husband to take very good care of me. He used the following words: "Omukwaate nk'ekirukwatika" meaning "Hold her as something precious that breaks easily."

Kachope took these words very seriously and treated me very well.

We blended in well with the rest of the village. I met many people who either belonged to my mother's clan of Abagweeri or that of my grandmother, Abasambu. These became my instant relatives and took care of me and my family. One market day, I was introduced to an old man called Omugurusi (Elder) Rwakaikara Araali who belonged to the Banyangabu clan, which is my very own. When we first got introduced to each other, he embraced me with such strength that after releasing me, I almost fell to the ground.

Omugurusi Rwakaikara Araali was a highly respected herbalist. He had medicine that cured many diseases. He sold it at the local market. The elderly gentleman adopted me into his family as his own daughter. He often visited our home and we also visited his. He lived with his son in the village next to ours. His wife had passed away the year before I met him. Going to the market was a source of relief for him. People who brought food to sell at the market made sure Omugurusi Rwakaikara Araali got fed first. He even took some left-overs home with him.

I saw in Mr. Rwakaikara what a daughter sees in a good father. He was kind, loving, gentle and generous. Like me, he too lost an entire family in the battle that took mine. He told me that originally he was from Burahya county and had relocated to Bunyangabu to do farm work. His family got captured when as a young man, he had gone on a hunting trip. The only relatives that survived were his aunt and uncle who lived in Busongora. They reunited many years after the battle was over.

While on the hunting trip, young Rwakaikara heard that the captors had invaded his village. He took off running and ended up in a place called Bugangaizi where he settled until the battle was over. Upon hearing of peace, he made it back to Burahya county where a kind couple adopted him. He learned how to build houses from his adopted father and eventually got married. He and his wife had five children. In his travels, Omugurusi Rwakaikara befriended people, animals and plants alike. He taught himself how to be an herbalist. Some of his children and their families later moved to Kampala city in search for better jobs.

WHERE DID MY PEOPLE GO?

MY HUSBAND'S DEPARTURE

One day, tragedy once again struck in my life. My husband left me while I was expecting our fourth daughter for a trip to Congo. I was in the fifth month of pregnancy when he left. As the days turned into weeks, and weeks into months, I never heard of his where- about. The children constantly asked me when their father was returning home. The family offered us comfort, saying that he would come back one day. We felt safe, at least for a while.

I carried the baby for four more months after my husband left for his final trip to Congo. When the time came to give birth, I felt the labor pains in the middle of the night. I sent my two daughters to go and inform my oldest brother-in-law and his wife Mangadaleena about the situation. They both quickly came to our house. My brother-in-law brought his bicycle with him. He, with the help of my two daughters and his wife lifted me up and placed me on the bicycle. He took me to the hospital while his wife took our three children to their house where they stayed until I returned from the hospital, with the baby.

My last-born baby was born at the local parish hospital. She and her brother were a little over six years apart. When I told the nuns about my husband's disappearance, they had a lot of sympathy for me. They had already heard about the tragedy of losing my family in battle. One of the foreign nuns said: "poor child." Although I did not speak English, I understood some common words and phrases. By saying "poor child," I did not know whether the nun was referring to me or the baby. Those nuns were so kind that they did not ask me to pay for the services at the hospital.

Upon returning home with the baby, the whole family was joyful. After three days, her grandmother named her Kabatalya. I am sure this name had a cultural meaning. I decided to take on its literal meaning which is "Child of Those Who Do Not Eat." I think the baby was given this name because it described our family situation. Ever since my husband's disappearance, food had become scarce in our home. I hardly had enough to feed my children, let alone me, an expectant mother.

At three months, Baby Kabatalya was baptized in the church. She was given the name Elizabeth. The nun who delivered her told me that my child reminded her of Elizabeth, the cousin of the Virgin Mary who gave birth to John the Baptist. She said that my child would possess great faith because she was born in hardship. Her father had disappeared while her mother's entire family had been lost in battle.

The nun assured me that people who endure a lot of hardships usually develop a strong character and do

GRANDMOTHER'S STORY

amazing things in life. She added that to bear and raise John the Baptist, the forerunner of Jesus Christ, Elizabeth had to be a strong woman of exceptional character. I took those words very seriously. The family welcomed the name Elizabeth which locally is pronounced as "Zabete."

As baby Kabatayla grew, there was no trace of her father. One man who usually went on trading trips with him did not know where he was either. They had parted company a few years earlier. My husband had decided to follow another route through the jungle where he met his fellow Congolese traders. His colleague, by the name of Mr. Kapere chose another route. He had decided to start trading in cloth and jewelry instead of hides and skins.

The year before my husband's disappearance, Mr. Kapere was ambushed by robbers who stole his merchandise and left him for dead. He was discovered by new traders who brought him home. Since then, he had given up trading in Congo. Instead, after recovering from his wounds, he travelled to Lake Katwe. There, he bought salt, returned home and sold it in surrounding markets.

The longer my husband stayed away, the more problems we faced. The workers who were helping us in the fields left because they were not being paid. My two oldest daughters and I started cultivating together. I carried the baby on my back and made a shade for her to stay in as we worked in the fields. When my son turned seven years old, he started taking care of the goats. Because our family funds had run out, I could no longer afford to pay a herder, or "omuliisa."

With my husband gone, the necessary home repairs were not done. The roof of our house started leaking. One day when the girls and I were at work in the fields, thieves broke into our home and stole all our valuable possessions. My son was out looking after the goats. We came home only to find pieces of broken pottery waiting for us. I wailed out loud as if a family member had just died.

My husband's departure caused so much pain to me that I thought of taking my children to the palace to live there. My in-laws also got very concerned about our situation. Not only was their son and brother missing, our family was falling apart. A family meeting was organized and it was decided that the best thing for me to do was to get married to my oldest brother-in-law. He would inherit the children and take care of us. Without any hesitation I answered "No." I did not want to become a second wife.

The decision not to marry my brother-in-law was also based on my love for Kachope. I constantly thought about him. I wondered what would happen if he returned one day only to find me married to his brother. I feared he would despise me as a weak wife who was unable to endure some hardship while awaiting her husband's return. Would I run back to him or not? Such thoughts caused me to have sleepless nights.

Although my children and I remained physically present in the compound, I was cut off from family affairs. I was viewed as a disobedient wife who had no respect for her in-laws. I was not invited to participate in family discussions. I became emotionally and psychologically isolated. Although my children continued playing with their cousins, their relationship was strained.

Refusing the marriage proposal was viewed as prideful behavior, taking myself to be higher than others. Even when my mother-in-law passed away two years later, I was almost treated as a guest. I was not invited to participate in the family ceremonies that surround death.

The source of comfort for me during my husband's absence was the church. There I rose to prominence. I was appointed guardian of the catechism children, the "Abaronde." As they gathered to be taught, I acted as their surrogate mother. Mind you, many came from non-Christian families. I had to interpret the lessons and assignments to them.

My own children, except the baby, were also enrolled in the Catechism classes. Although I had no formal education and could hardly read or write, I received informal education through the church, just as I had at the palace. I even sang church hymns as though I could read the words. Some of them were in Latin.

The church also gave me prominence by putting me in charge of opening and locking the Virgin Mary's house. This is the small house on the side of the church where a statue of the Mother of Jesus is housed. Opening and closing this house was a job for the nuns. When I was appointed to this task, I felt as though I had been lifted up to heaven. In humility and gratitude, I kept on asking myself: "Who am I to receive this honor?"

As problems at home got worse, the nuns enrolled my

son and last-born daughter in school. I worked very hard to find school fees for my son. Daughter Kabatalya attended school for free. She obtained a scholarship from school. The two oldest girls were already too old for primary school. Like me, what they learned was from Catechism classes. They continued working in the fields with me.

Daughter Herena was very intelligent. She had a strong sense of imagination and curiosity. The nuns who worked at the hospital often invited her to help them run errands. As a result, she developed skills in midwifery. She also liked to help people recover from illnesses. That's how she gradually developed interest in finding herbs to cure illnesses.

We sold off all the goats that we had so that my son could go to school. He also served as an altar boy during mass. Although he too was beyond first grade at the time of enrollment, the school principal made an exception. He had a small and short build. His size allowed him to look younger than his age.

My son went to school for four years. He learned how to read and write before dropping out. He was already fifteen years old by fourth grade. After dropping out of school, he went to live with Omugurusi Rwakaikara Araali whose sons taught him how to build houses. He also started earning some money building houses.

Although I went through a lot of pain during my husband's absence, I remained very strong in public and in front of my children. Besides praying, I always told myself proverbs that I had learned from the elders. Before going to work in the fields, I told myself the proverb: "Omugara agyaayo taburwa nsambu." This proverb encourages hard work by saying that even a lazy person who cultivates, has a piece of land where the harvest comes from. This provides land for the next season.

Another reason why I remained looking strong, beautiful and attractive is that I wore very beautiful clothes. My husband always brought me beautiful fabric called "Kitenge" from his trips to Congo. He also had good taste in selecting jewelry. I was also one of the few village women, besides the nuns who wore shoes. I had a pair of slippers that made the noise "tap, tap, tap" as I walked. I was told that these were called "Sapatu" in Swahili.

My baby daughter, Kabatalya excelled in school. She performed very well in every subject, including music and sports. Her physical beauty and good personality added to her popularity. Sister Beatrice loved her so much that she sewed clothes for her. She often remarked that little Elizabeth was the child she never had. At her first communion, the nun made her little friend a white dress with wings that made her look like an angel. The nuns also gave her some white shoes. Following mass, my husband's family prepared a big feast and invited many people. Some of the nuns, including her best friend Sister Beatrice attended the party.

My son often came to visit us from Omugurusi Rwakaikara Araali's house during the weekends. From the little money that he made, he was able to bring us special food including bread, rice, salt and sugar. He also left me with some money to buy Kerosene so that we could light our lamps at night.

One day, heavy rain fell that was accompanied by hail and wind. These forces caused our house to fall to the ground. I faced a new challenge of having to build a house, something I had never done before. My brothers-in-law could not help because they had relocated to Kampala, the capital. They went there in search of better jobs and usually came home during the Christmas holidays. My father-in-law was getting too old to build houses.

I built the grass houses called "Ekisu." with the help of my children. My son usually placed the central pole, held on to it, while his sisters and I built the circular structure around the pole. We dug deep holes, installed the poles and covered the holes with soil. We made sure that the house foundation was firm and strong.

Besides rain, hail and wind, we tried to build houses that were strong enough to withstand hyenas. These fierce animals liked to visit our home in the evenings when we gathered around the fire. We heard them scratching and tearing on the house. Afraid and trembling, the children huddled around me. I gathered them to myself as a hen gathers her chicks under her wings in time of danger. Early in the morning, we opened the door only to find hyena footprints on the ground and holes in the house walls. We automatically knew that repair work had to begin immediately. Thank God most of these wild animals have been tamed in national parks.

For two years, I went through the process of building

houses that kept on falling. To be exact, my children and I built four houses in that short period of time. I decided to share my predicament with Mother Superior at the convent. After much prayer and consulting with her colleagues, she gave me and my children an offer of a house close to the church. It was a house that had been built for orphans. The project had been discontinued because another parish decided to take it on. We were very grateful. On the first day when we moved into the house, the nuns prepared a very big feast for us. It is called "kutaaha enju" which is translated as "entering the house."

At the time when I was given the church house, my last-born daughter had just been admitted into Kinyamasika Teacher-Training College. Mass was celebrated at our new home. Prayers were offered to God requesting our protection. Our new home at the parish was two and a half miles from our old house.

Katalina, Herena and I walked that distance daily to go and work in the fields. Despite this challenge, we felt safe, protected and grateful. At the church, I was promoted to leading prayer in the Virgin Mary's house. Whenever the faithful came searching for a miracle, I was available to pray for them. I did this during the weekends because during weekdays, my daughters and I went to the fields.

The requests to the Virgin Mary were many and varied. The most frequent ones included the need for a baby, a bountiful harvest, a wife or a husband. Some people came requesting a cure from an illness. Many women came to the Virgin Mary requesting that their husbands remain faithful to them. They often used the expression, "Please let not my husband look at another woman."

Although our lives had improved, I still missed my husband very much. The children often talked about him, especially when they saw other children with their fathers. My dream of having a large family with ten children vanished. I nonetheless never gave up hope that one day Kachope would return to us.

After living in the church house for one year, I received more shocking news. My second daughter, Herena had conceived a baby with a man called Antonio. He was not the kind of man that was ready to settle down with one wife. At the news, I did not know whether to be angry or to celebrate the coming of a grandchild. Instead, I went to the Virgin Mary's house to pray and was granted peace.

At this time, King Kyebambe had departed from this earth. Before his death, he had instructed his relatives never to forget about me. Mr. Joseph Kairumba, one of the King Kyebambe's relatives had heard of my husband's disappearance. One Sunday after mass, he talked to me and invited me to move to Burungu Village. He promised to give me a piece of land called "Mairu" which belonged to the king. Without any hesitation, I accepted the offer. I started planning the move which took place two months following Mr. Kairumba's offer.

MOVE TO BURUNGU VILLAGE

I welcomed the move from Kinyamasika to Burungu with open arms. I felt happy and protected to be reuniting with my family that my father, King Kyebambe left me with. I was very relieved to know that my first grandchild would be born on our own land, in our own home. I was also pleased to know that my work with the nuns was going to continue because I would be in the same parish. I would just have to walk about a mile longer to the parish than I did previously.

When my son Erikanjeru came to visit us, I told him the news about the coming move to Burungu. He jumped up and down, thanking God for the favor. Rightaway, he told me that he would build the family house with the help of Burungu people and Omugurusi Rwakaikara Araali's family members.

Before the move to Burungu, my son got together a team of well-wishers who built for us a beautiful, strong house known as "ekibandahooli." Instead of being round like ekisu, this type of house has a roof with two sides to it. It resembled the house that my husband built for us when we got married. This was a major upgrade from the houses my children and I buil in Kinyamasika after my husband's departure.

The nuns and my in-laws had mixed feelings about our leaving Kinyamasika. On one hand, they were glad that we were joining family members who would take care of us. On the other, they did not want us to leave the Kinyamasika community. My father-in-law who had advanced in age feared that he might never see his grandchildren again. After his son's departure, he always feared that I would get married to another man, thereby allowing his grandchildren to be raised in another family, belonging to another clan.

I always assured my father-in-law that getting married to another man was out of question for me. I told him that if Kachope did not return to me here on earth, we would meet in heaven. I vowed to remain single as long as I lived. Although he believed me, he was still skeptical. He wished I had chosen to remain in the family by getting married to my brother-in-law.

When the work of building our new house was complete, my son came and told us. We packed all our belongings, ready to leave for Burungu. I took the children to go and say farewell to their grandfather and other relatives. While a few shed tears about our departure, others were glad about the move. One of my husband's nephews was happy at the news that our former homestead and land were being given to him by his grandfather.

Mr. Joseph Kairumba was a very prominent man. Besides being a veterinary officer, he farmed many acres

GRANDMOTHER'S STORY

of land and owned cattle. After getting married to his hard-working wife, the family became very successful business people. They even had some cattle from abroad and introduced a new kind of banana known as "Kitika." They supplied milk and food to local schools, hospitals, prisons and a host of other places. Mrs Olive Kairumba Abwoli even drove a lorry, something that surprised many local people, especially women. She was a pioneer in many ways.

On the day of our move, Mr. Kairumba sent a lorry to move us. It was driven by a paid driver. We loaded the lorry, ready to leave for our new home. The nuns, priests and some parishioners came to pray for us and to say goodbye. My daughter Kabatalya came with us but returned to the house at the parish the next day. She lived there with three other girls until after completing her teacher-training education.

When we moved to Burungu, I was in my early fifties. I became the family matriarch. All family responsibilities, including the naming of babies fell upon my shoulders. We arrived in Burungu and found many people waiting to welcome us. They brought with them plenty of drinks which included water and banana juice. A few men brought to us banana beer. Upon seeing this drink, my son whispered to the chief to let him know that our family did not drink alcohol. The chief made the announcement regarding this matter. From then on, our family was given the name "Abarokole" meaning "The Saved Ones."

The chief, whose name was Buraara requested the

men to help my son unload the lorry. He also requested the women to help me place the household items in their proper places. The whole night was full of celebration to welcome us to our new village. I also gained instant relatives. They either belonged to my mother's clan of Bagweeri or my grandmother's of Basambu. There were also a few people from Mr. Kairumba's clan of Basiita who came to help us re-settle in Burungu. Chief Buraara belonged to this clan. Surprisingly, I did not meet anyone from my clan of Banyangabu or that of my children, Bayaga. In that sense, one can say that we were transplants.

As soon as my children and I got settled in Burungu, we started farming. We had enough land on which to grow crops to feed us. Before harvesting our own crops, some kind-hearted people brought us raw food including, millet, potatoes, bananas and beans. My two daughters and I also did farm work for other people who paid us with food.

My son often found short-term work called "Laija-Laija" building houses. Sometimes he was called to Omugurusi Rwakaikara Araali's village for work that lasted a few months. He had bought a bicycle which he rode to get him there. He spent most of the money he made on our family.

Three months after moving to Burungu, my daughter Herena gave birth to a baby boy that I named "Byaruhanga" which can be translated as "Everything belongs to God." He was baptized and received the name George which the local people pronounce as "Zolizi." He also got Empaako of "Adyeri." Byaruhanga was born a very tall

GRANDMOTHER'S STORY

baby and continued going up, up and up. By his teenage years, he had grown up to seven feet. Villagers gave him the nick-name "Mulengwa" meaning "Tall." Every time he attempted to enter a house, he had to bend.

On Byaruhanga's first birthday, my first daughter, Katalina got married to Chief Buraara. During the same year, my last-born daughter completed her teacher-training program and moved to Burungu. She started teaching primary school. We lived in the same house until her brother built his own house next-door to ours. He got married but unfortunately lost his wife during child-birth. He named his baby boy "Aliganyira" meaning "God Will Have Mercy." Aliganyira received the Empaako of Akiiki. Following his mother's death, Herena and Kabatalya brought baby Aliganyira home. He got baptized and was given the name John which locally is known as "Yohana."

Within a very short time, my family grew by two more members. The little boys, George Byaruhanga Adyeri and John Aliganyira Akiiki were a welcome addition to my family. When my last-born daughter Kabatalya got married, her sister Herena and I worked together to provide for these boys who were less than two years apart. We continued providing for our family until she too got married to a man of Mbuzi village. After that, I became the sole provider for my family.

When Kabatalya got married, she had to leave her teaching job to become a full-time house wife. Unfortunately, her marriage did not last beyond three years. She was a modern woman who did not fit well into the traditional marriage structure. Her husband loved to drink alcohol which activity was followed by having an eye for women. His wife was expected to tolerate this behavior as "normal" and "acceptable". She was expected to cook, clean after him, bear children and do farm work. Her mother-in-law had told her thus: "If a man sees other women, this does not mean that he does not love you."

  My daughter heard these words through one ear but they left through another. She wondered how a loving spouse could continue living a single life after marriage and claim to be loving his/her partner. She chose to disobey her mother-in-law's instructions. I think my daughter had taken my own marriage story seriously. I had told her that Kachope, her father was very loving and faithful to me.

  I constantly advised my daughter to work hard and save her marriage. She already had two baby girls that were born fifteen months apart. Some of her devout catholic friends encouraged her to stay in her marriage, even at the risk of death. One of her friends told her that if she died to save her marriage, she might be considered a martyr for married women. She might even become a saint.

  My daughter remained in her marriage until one day the worst happened. One of her husband's lovers plotted to poison her so that she could take over her husband. When Kabatalya discovered the plot, she decided to leave, taking her younger daughter called Kajumba Abwoli with her. Our whole family welcomed her brave decision. The two of them came to Burungu to live with us. Her first-

GRANDMOTHER'S STORY

born daughter called Kabadooka Amooti remained with her father. She was raised by her step-mother. In her twenties, she also came to live in Burungu with us until she eventually got married.

After Kabatalya's marriage ended, she decided to go back to her teaching profession. Kabatalya had no choice but to accept teaching appointments that were far away from us. During this period, she met a gentleman from Mwenge county of Bagaya clan. He was a fellow teacher. Before long, together they had a baby girl. Immediately, I felt a special spiritual bond with this baby. I named her Kabagarama, the name of the house at the palace where I grew up.

Before returning to teaching, my daughter had to make a major decision regarding the care of her two children. She had to make a choice between taking both of them with her or leaving the baby with me. Finally, she decided to leave the baby with me, taking the older one, who was ready for school, with her. Since the age of two years, baby Kabagarama, whose Empaako is Akiiki became my very own child.

I carried Kabagarama on my back to the fields, fed her and took care of her as any good mother would. My relationship with her changed from that of grandmother to one of mother. This baby became my confidant, someone with whom I could share my life story. I needed someone to listen to me without judging me.

Whenever sadness surrounded me, this child became my comforter, a shoulder to cry on. When I posed the question; "Where did my people go?", Kabagarama gave me a listening ear. The two of us became gifts to each other. I adopted her into my life and she also adopted me into hers. Deep down, I knew this was the baby that "fell on my arm." This statement indicates that Kabagarama was sent to me by God as an answer to prayer.

The villagers respected me and often called upon me for advice. When conflict arose in any home, I was the first one to be invited to settle it. The people knew me as a very fair person who had a blend of traits that made me a natural leader. I was firm, disciplined, tender and humble. I befriended rulers and everyday common people alike. I did not do any work without first praying and asking God for help in making the right decision.

My connections with the church and the palace gave me a lot of self-confidence that was sometimes mistaken to be a display of arrogance. Those people who got to know me found me to be a very loving and kind human being. If I did boast at all, it is because I was expressing gratitude to God. Because my children and I were new to Burungu village, some people thought our family had come from the sky. Women of our family were often called "Abahumakati", meaning "the Royal ones."

Many villagers admired me for my ability to pray for people and obtain positive results. They also envied me for my being in company with the nuns at the convent. They were called "Ababikira" or Sisters. Some villagers asked me if I spoke foreign languages which they imitated as "fifififfi." I told them that I knew very little English. I had picked up a few words from the palace, the church and my daughter, the school teacher.

My daughters and I were weavers of baskets, mats and cloth. We decorated pots, calabashes and anything else that crossed our paths. This activity is called "okuhunda." We also had very beautiful voices and often sang in harmony. Besides church songs, we sang the traditional songs known as "Enanga." The process of singing these songs is called: "kuteere enanga."

My son was a hunter, just like my own maternal uncle. He and his friends often left for hunting trips that lasted several months. At the end of the hunting season, they brought home roasted buffalo meat. They did not hunt other animals such as antelopes and lions. Many people, including my family members belong to the antelope clan. Destroying the life of an antelope is compared to destroying the life of a relative. The lion is equated with rulership of our kingdom. The king's title is "Entale Ya Tooro" meaning "Lion of Tooro." The precious lion receives great honor and is protected.

After my son's first wife died, he mourned for a very long time. He married another wife after three years. The family moved to Bwamba, a region on a higher elevation of mount Rwenzori. It is very close to Congo. His reason for moving so far away was to find fertile land near the top of Mount Rwenzori. Family members suspected that he was moving closer to the area where his father had disappeared, hoping that one day, he would be able to find him. Although we were all sad at his departure, we prayed for the family and let them go. Occasionally, he visited us and brought us very sweet mangoes.

I took advantage of my connections with the sisters, especially Mother Superior. I threatened to report men who beat their wives to this powerful nun. One day, I was called to the home of a man in the neighboring village called Kiguma. The man's name was "Musaijamubi" which is translated as "Badman." I don't know whether this was his birth name or he got it because of his cruelty toward his wife. Whenever he got drunk, he quarreled with his wife and often beat her. Some people said this man beat his wife as though she was his drum.

I walked a long distance to Kiguma village with my granddaughter Kabagarama who was about ten years old then. Upon arrival at Musaijamubi's home, the man was seated in his compound with a circle of friends drinking some type of locally-brewed drink known as "Kagogo." This drink is known as having the ability to "fry" people's brains.

When the men saw me, some ran away while others attempted to hide the alcohol. Without greeting anyone, I hit the ground several times with my cane. I gave a long speech to Musaijamubi, saying: "Musaijamubi, I am ashamed of you. Why do you beat your wife? She bore seven children and cooks for you every day. What is wrong with you? I thought after you got baptized by Faza (Father), you would become a good man. You still act like Omukafiiri (a pagan). I am going to report you to Faza on Sunday and to the head Sister. When she comes here, you will see how your compound will shake as though an earthquake is passing through."

As I spoke, Musaijamubi and his remaining friends looked down. They were too afraid to look at my furious eyes. After the speech, my granddaughter and I left for home. From then on, Musaijamubi's wife Bajwaaha which means "They Get Tired" never got any other beating. Peace returned to that home. People in the village started saying that my magical words sent out fire balls that chased away evil spirits. Upon hearing these words, I often twisted my neck and pointed up to God in heaven.

Besides resolving conflicts and praying for people, I was a very good storyteller. Two years following our move to Burungu, I was invited to join the Elders Club of storytellers. This was an elite group that was made up of people who were considered to be carriers of traditional wisdom. Most of them were grandparents, over sixty years of age.

Once in a while, a younger person who possessed unique talent and skills in the arts was invited to join the Elders Club. These special skills include music, dancing, spiritual healing, comedy, drumming and storytelling. Young people were taught proper behavior by utilizing these skills. Even some older people who for one reason or another had missed this learning process got an opportunity to catch up on these important lessons.

My association with people at the palace made me even more popular and powerful in the village. During the special celebration known as "Empango", my family and I went to the palace and participated. This occasion was a commemoration of the king's coronation. We danced the special royal dance known as "Amakondere." We also attended services at the Protestant Cathedral during these special occasions.

I shared many stories with my granddaughter Kabagarama. I usually invited her to my bed so that she could get warm, especially during the rainy days in Tooro. My stories educated her about life issues, comforted me during sad times and gave me hope for the future. I had no doubt that this little girl was sent to me by God. I needed someone to confide in so that my unique story would never die. I taught her storytelling skills so that she might one day tell our family story.

I possessed royalty that was also heavenly. I often spoke about God in a very intimate and personal way. I kept my children in church. On Sundays, I often stayed at church for many hours. After mass, I opened the Virgin Mary's house to let in people who needed extra prayer. Kabagarama was always beside me. We took packed lunch of roasted potatoes, cassava, maize and plantain with us. On some special Sundays, the nuns invited us to the convent for lunch.

It's amazing how I was obeyed by humans and other creatures alike. I never got bitten by snakes or stray dogs. Even the lion that once in a while came out to warm himself never bothered me and my family. This majestic creature came out about three times a year and sat on a stone to absorb some sunshine. I had been instructed by the elders to pass the lion quietly and respectfully when I saw him. They told me that he was kin to us and would never harm us.

The only creature that disobeyed me was the male goat called Rutanga. This goat was strange, stubborn and difficult to tame. He had a long beard and chased after both food and females. As soon as he was released from his shed, Rutanga ran very fast in search of these treasures.

One day, I let the goats out of their shed before leaving for the field. The other goats obeyed my commands except Rutanga. They did not run off or roam around without my permission. I held onto Rutanga's rope, suspecting that he might run off. My granddaughter Kabagarama was right behind me. Both of us were afraid of this wild goat.

On this beautiful, sunny day, Rutanga did the unthinkable. When I opened the goat shed, the stubborn goat headed out very fast. I tried to hold on to his rope but the goat kept on running. During the chase, I fell and my dress was pulled up. When I turned around, I remember seeing my granddaughter cover her eyes in shame because she had seen my nakedness.

At that moment, I prayed to God to forgive Rutanga for what he had done. I even made the sign of the cross. Kabagarama, who was about nine years old then, ran to my help. She grabbed the rope from my hand and tied it to a near-by tree. Her act of bravery stopped the goat from running away from us. I got up from the fall, wiped the dust off my body and continued on with my duties.

When daughter Kabatalya returned home for the holidays, we reported Rutanga to her. She was so upset that she decided to sell him off. She also hired one of the village boys to take care of the goats. The boy instantly became a member of our family. He lived with his grandfather after losing both of his parents and grandmother to smallpox. His name was "Kafuuzi" which means "orphan". He was about twelve years old when he became a part of our family and stayed with us for six years until he got married.

I named the young man "Kisembo" meaning "Gift." My entire family played a major role during his wedding. I became his adopted grandmother and Kabatalya became his adopted mother. My son was the head negotiator or Kibonabuko when the young man visited his future bride's family to announce himself and to engage in the conversation regarding bride wealth.

By the time Kisembo got married, Kabatalya had moved back to live with us. She also had another baby, a son called Kyaligonza with Empaako of Amooti. His name Kyaligonza means: " Whatever God Wants is Alright." He was given the baptism name of Francis. This was during the time when the country was going through preparations for independence from Britain.

We were very happy at Kabatalya's return home. We all called her Ateenyi, her Empaako. She started teaching at Nyansozi primary school, a few miles away from home. She bought a bicycle and rode to school. The bicycle brought her mixed blessings. On one hand, she was admired for riding a bicycle that was supposed to be for men only. Some villagers called her "Omungereeza or Omujungu", meaning "Someone from Europe." On the other hand, some other people feared that she might grow a beard and attempt to beat up men, which act would be taboo. Besides riding the bicycle, brave Kabatalya whistled, engaging in yet another behavior set aside for men.

Upon her return, daughter Kabatalya built us a larger, more modern house. The roof of this house had four sides and was covered with corrugated iron. It also had wooden doors and windows. Our home was located downhill, close to the stream and well from where we fetched water. The only problem was that when it rained as it often did during the months of March and September, falling rain kept us awake at night. The rain drops and the often-accompanying hail fell hard on the roof. The good thing is that the roof never leaked. We stayed dry and comfortable.

Rain gave us clean water to drink. We collected it in a large tank and later poured it in our drinking water clay pot known as "ensoha." Kabatalya, who many people called "Omwegesa" or "Omusomesa" meaning "Teacher", had very clean habits. She distilled our drinking water and kept it covered. The water we fetched from the well was boiled first and distilled before we drank it.

Our home was very strong and beautiful until the year 1960 when the earthquake "Omusisa" caused it a lot of damage. This earthquake was so strong that it caused the Cathedral of Virika Parish to completely crumble. A whole new church with a round structure was built.

Although our home did not completely fall to the ground, the walls cracked in several areas. Even sections of the roof started leaking which caused damage to the floor and the foundation. Our family and many neighbors who experienced damage to their homes became very sad.

Since the 1960 earthquake, we lived in fear of being visited by another one. Tremors were a constant reminder that this ordeal had come to stay. Although I feared the possible return of another big earthquake, I did not display my fear in public. I was strong and reminded people to pray. I constantly recited my rosary and sang church songs.

I constantly worried about my granddaughter Kabagarama leaving me one day. By the time her mother returned to Burungu, my little girl was attending Mugusu Primary School, which was for girls only. Her two cousins, Byaruhanga and Aliganyira did not live with us all the time. Aliganyira was attending secondary school and came home just during the holidays. Byaruhanga worked in carpentry with Frere (Brother in French) at the parish and came home occasionally to visit us. Since the villagers did not speak French, the Brother at the parish was called "Fuleera."

At Mugusu Primary School, Kabagarama excelled in her studies. I often heard her mother say that the next step was for her daughter to enroll in St. Anne's Junior School after completing the sixth grade. Since Saint Anne's was a boarding school, that meant she would have to leave home. Although I wanted to cling on to her and keep her at home with me, I wished her well. I wanted her to go, explore the world, visit other lands and one day tell my story, our family story.

SECRET PLACE IN THE WOODS

Those of us who lost our loved ones in battle knew each other and bonded together. We belonged to several villages and called ourselves "Ababanyagwa" meaning "Those Who Belong to the Captives." It was our secret language. Another name we called ourselves was "Basigara" meaning, "Those Who Remain." We defined our kinship by saying, "esagama enunkire" meaning "blood has smelt among us." This is a very strong statement that is used to describe a situation in which relatives who have been separated for a long time get reunited.

There was a place that we the survivors visited to reconnect with our departed family members. I was first told about this place by Omugurusi Rwakaikara Araali. I could not go there at that time because I had small children to take care of. When we moved to Burungu, the preacher at the local church also told me about this unique place where the battle survivors assembled. I decided to start attending.

The visits to the special place in the woods lasted all day. At every visit, new people joined the group and some old ones did not return. Most of those who left relocated to the capital city in search for jobs. Some of the younger ones got married and moved away to other villages. Some new ones joined us due to marriage while others intentionally relocated to jon our group. They came in search of community, to join people who shared their stories.

This special place was kept a secret from those who did not share our experience. It was deep in the woods, hidden behind a cave. There we gathered to mourn the departed and to assure them that we would never forget them. It was also a place where we comforted each other, shared our strengths and received advice on how to address a variety of issues.

The cave

During these gatherings, marital and other disputes were settled by the elders who had plenty of wisdom.

Some lucky young men and women sometimes caught the eye of a potential mate. However, they were not allowed to display their desires at these meetings. They had to get permission from the elders upon returning home.

The elders always reminded us to never forget our unique story. They told us to pass it on from one generation to the next. These words never departed from me. I made the decision to pass on this story to my child or grandchild that God would give me to keep the secret trust.

There were two visits a year to the secret place. Both were during harvest seasons so that plenty of food could be taken to share with the departed relatives. The major visit took place during the December-January season when millet, which is the main staple food of the people had just been harvested. The ancestors needed to taste the fresh harvest of millet known as "omuherya."

The June-July trip to the woods did not require too much preparation because the crops of the season are not as prestigious as millet. They include maize, beans, peas, potatoes, and cassava. During these trips, we also took chicken and goat meat with us. On both trips, we took with us banana juice, known as "ensande." and water in drinking gourds. We did not take any alcoholic beverages, not even the local brew of banana beer. We did not want the ancestors to find us intoxicated.

Many of us who visited the secret place were Christians, baptized in the church. Christianity was very appealing to us. We identified with Jesus Christ who died and rose again. This gave us hope of seeing our loved ones again.

We were also sure that Jesus and his family loved us because we were in a similar situation of having been separated from our loved ones in a cruel manner.

The church leaders who came with us often lead prayers at these meetings. Among those who attended frequently was the local Catholic church leader. His church-given or baptism name was Gabriel which the villagers pronounce as "Gabudieri". We recited the Rosary and together sang church songs. My favorite song was and is still "Guma, Guma; Yezu Niyo Mpeera." This song is translated as, "Be Strong, Be Strong: Jesus is the Reward." I love this song very much. Singing it gives me strength to go through each single day. We also sang some hymns from the Protestant tradition. I liked best the one called "Kansiime." which talked about being grateful to Jesus who washed our sins away.

For Christians, the December-January period had a special meaning. People celebrated the coming of the Savior and the new life in Christ. This was also a season to celebrate babies and families. Babies born during this season received special names such as "Mugisa" meaning "Blessing"; "Kisembo", meaning "Gift", or "Kabasinguzi," meaning "Child of Victorious People." In addition, those babies born into Christian families received names such as Christopher, Christine, Joseph, Emmanuel, and Angel. Their local equivalents are "Kulisitofa", "Kulisitiina", "Yozeefu", "Manueri" and "Malaika".

The waterfall

Besides the cave, our secret place in the woods had a waterfall. Like River Kanywankoko, the waterfall had drums beating all the time. The drums were sometimes accompanied by songs. The drums were particularly loud during the season of harvesting millet and when the big star appeared in the sky above. The name of honor for this star is "Nyamuha-Ibona; Enganzi y'Okweezi." Its literal translation is "Rewarder of the One who Sees; Favored One of the Moon."

Children who are born during the appearance of the special star are very fortunate. Such fortunate people are often told "Okazaarwa Kweezi nayoga" meaning that they were born during the special time when the moon was "taking a bath." They are considered to possess special gifts of healing and prophesy. They often exhibit great wisdom and knowledge. They are regarded as ambassadors from the Bachwezi, the ancient rulers of the land.

There is another mystery that surrounds the place where we went to meet our departed relatives. There are formations on the wall of the cave that look like breasts of a woman. A milk-like substance is seen dripping from these breast-like structures called "Amabeere Ga Nyina Mwiiru" translated as the "Breasts of the Mother of the Slave/Servant." The breasts are believed to belong to a

Amabeere

GRANDMOTHER'S STORY

mother who left her child behind. This grieving mother left behind some milk to feed her child and the children of other mothers who vanished. These mysterious structures are a constant reminder that mothers had been separated from their nursing babies.

I tried my very best not to miss trips to meet our departed loved ones. Apart from the festivities of the day and the food that was brought from many homes, I liked very much to hear the survival stories that people shared. This activity usually took place at around noon, when the sun was directly above us. This was an indication that God, Kazooba-Nyamuhanga, translated as "Ray of the Sun-Creator," was speaking directly to and through us.

We usually got to the cave very early in the morning, before sunrise. We lit lanterns to provide light deep in the woods. The day's activities began with people greeting one another. This was followed by prayers, songs and drumming. Some time was devoted to mourning and remembering the departed.

From the north side of the cave came angel-like beings that were dressed in white from head to toe that joined us. They spoke in whispers and no one touched them because they were from the spirit world. They waved their hands as a way of greeting us.

The angel-like beings sat on an anthill that was to the east of us, in the direction of the rising sun called "burugaizooba." We all sat together and listened to current events that were taking place in the different villages. These included happy events such as marriages, births and the harvest. There were also reports of sad events such as deaths, crop failures and family conflicts.

Once everyone who had a report to present had done so, the moderator who was an elder closed the discussion. At this point, the ancestors went back to the other side of the cave from which they had come. Special servers were sent there to serve them food and drinks.

We usually ate between 10 am and 11.30 am. As noon approached, all those people who were wearing hats and head wraps removed them so that they could receive wisdom and understanding. The departed ancestors returned to the anthill. They were usually about twenty in number. The number among us usually fluctuated between forty and fifty. The elders among us who had gray hair sat in a separate section to receive honor. It is the belief that with each gray hair comes a spark of wisdom.

Couples and their young children sat together. Female and male youth sat separately in order to avoid any temptation of getting involved with each other. This place was secret and sacred. God visited us in a unique way and brought back those from the spirit world to speak to us. There was no room whatsoever for romantic ventures.

One of the lessons I learned at our gatherings is that the survivors came from different backgrounds. Besides those of us who survived the battle between the kings of Bunyoro and Tooro, there were others who escaped from the captors that came from very far in the east. These captors had pale-looking skin. They were believed to have come from underneath the ocean. Those who perished during

GRANDMOTHER'S STORY

these times are believed to have been taken away to far-off places in large ships. The captors' weapons roared and made the earth shake.

Although the kings and chiefs put up a lot of resistance against these invaders who were tying up the people in chains and taking them away, their efforts were often in vain. Their weapons were no match. These strangers spoke foreign languages. They appeared to be hungry and thirsty all the time. We were told that they sometimes drained blood out of people's bodies and drank it.

During the time when people shared their survival stories, we all listened very intensely. Those who had coughs tried hard to suppress them. No wonder mothers who were nursing babies and had small children were not welcome to these meetings. It was feared that the crying babies would become a source of distraction during these solemn moments.

People asked me to share my survival story over and over again. The loss of my sister Kabalinzi to the snake bite and Basemera who disappeared without any trace caused many people to shed tears. I also listened very attentively as others told their stories of loss and survival. One of the stories that I think about all the time was told by a man whose grandfather had escaped from captivity by the strangers from the east. As the captives walked chained to one another, he managed to unchain himself without the captors noticing. Being from a long line of metal workers known as "abaheesi", he possessed unique powers breaking metal. His given name was "Rwabaheesi" which means "Belonging to Metal-Workers."

Upon appealing to his power, Rwabaheesi broke the chain that had bound him. He took off running in the opposite direction and ended up drowning in a large river. Those chasing after him gave up, being convinced that he would die in the massive water. While in the water, he ended up being swallowed by a crocodile. Because of his tall body of about seven feet, the crocodile was not able to swallow him. The large animal climbed up to the river bank and spat out the young man who was about twenty years old.

When Rwabaheesi opened his eyes, he saw the large animal lying near him, ready to open his mouth and swallow him again. Without wasting any time, the young man took off running. He continued running until he arrived at a house with smoke. This was an indication that human beings were around. He sought help from the residents of the home who directed him toward his village. After a journey lasting a month, he returned home. Along the way, he was fed and offered shelter by strangers.

Another survivor story that caught my attention was that of twins who were captured together in the same battle that took my people. They were captured separately at ten years of age and taken to foreign lands. There they lived as servants. The people they lived with spoke foreign languages and ate strange foods. Deep in their hearts, each twin longed to see her sister. They prayed day and night to be reunited one day.

When the twins were about twelve years old, it came about that strange beings that were believed to be evil spirits started passing through villages and setting people's houses on fire. As both girls slept in their homes in different villages, their homes were set on fire during the same night. Just the twins survived separately and started running from their captivity. Not aware of the direction they followed, the two girls ran toward their village.

While on the run, the twins were looked after by strangers who welcomed them into their homes and fed them. Some kind parents invited them to stay several days with them so that they could rest and regain energy for their journey. The girls had not forgotten the name of their village, their parents' names and their clan name. They were Basambu, just like my grandmother. This photographic memory helped them to not only re-unite with each other but also return to their village.

Each twin was adopted by clan relatives in the same village, on opposite sides of a hill. Their story was told everywhere, hoping someone would find a surviving family member. Two young traders took it upon themselves to find some relatives of these girls. They went back to their own village and spread the good news. Before long, an old couple related to the twins' father was found. The couple lived close to the top of the hill. They begged the traders to bring the twins home.

The traders visited the twins' adoptive parents and shared the news of their relatives who lived close to the top of the hill. They all agreed that before their return, the precious girls would need to meet at the market so that many people could witness their return. The twins were fifteen years old then.

On the next market day, the two adoptive parents took the twin girls to the market. Upon seeing each other, there was joy mixed with sorrow. The twins embraced each other with tears and laughter. They had been separated for five years!! Many other people cried, laughed, danced, screamed and did some ulation. They had just witnessed a miracle. The girls who had been considered dead for five years, had returned to life.

That day, the two traders, the adoptive parents and many other people from the marked accompanied the twins to their new home. The whole village gathered to celebrate the return of the twins who had been declared dead but were now alive. There was great celebration at the home that was close to the top of the hill. The twins remained together with their relatives until they each got married.

The story of the twins who "returned from death" always amazed us. It also confirmed to me the belief that twins are inseparable. My mother told me that what happens to one twin usually happens to the other. Parents of twins are considered to have a double blessing. She also told me that twins receive equal treatment. They are fed at the same time and equal amounts of food. In time of trouble, they receive similar and equal punishment. When they behave well, they are rewarded equally.

There is fear that if twins are treated differently, one of them might die. The death of a twin is called "Kuguruka" or "Jumping." The birth of twins into the family changes the whole family forever. Fathers of twins are called "Isa-

GRANDMOTHER'S STORY

barongo" which means "Father of Twins". The mother's name changes to "Nyinabarongo" which means "Mother of Twins."

The twins also receive special names that distinguish them from other people. The male twin who is born first is called "Isingoma" and the one who is born second is called "Kato." The twin girl who arrives first is called "Nyangoma" and the second arrival is called "Nyakato." The babies in the family, both nuclear and extended who are born after twins also receive special names. When you hear a name such as "Kiiza" or "Kahwa," you know there are twins in the family.

At our meetings in the secret place, time of sharing was followed by more eating, singing and dancing. The drummers among us made sure our drum, "Engoma" spoke loudly and clearly. Our guests stayed with us for as long as they could and enjoyed the festivities. After blessing us, they left and returned in the direction where they came from. As evening approached, we cleaned our meeting place, packed our belongings and returned to our respective homes.

Upon returning from the visit with our departed ancestors, we were very joyful. It was as though we had received new lives. We displayed renewed energy and great hope for the future. When we got home, there was a big feast at one of the homes that was marked with dancing and singing. Young men and women preparing for marriage were announced. The elders also shared news from the ancestors. During these gatherings, disputes were settled and peace returned to the villages.

Not all descendants of the captured joined in the

trips to the secret place. Some had been left as babies and those who adopted them decided to keep their story hidden from them due to fear of rejection. Most of them feared that if their true stories were revealed, family disruptions would occur. A common proverb that was said in these situations was; "Ebikara omunda bisemeza amalembo" which means; "Things that are unexposed clear the paths."

I am glad I participated in these reunions. They provided me with strength and gave me and my children an extended family. I was convinced that in times of trouble or if I needed help, I could count on these people. We attended these meetings until the area drew the attention of visitors, mainly from foreign lands. After discontinuing the visits to the secret place, our relationships did not end. We continued visiting each other in different homes, particularly during important occasions such as weddings, funerals and naming ceremonies.

THE 60s DECADE

During the 1960s, our family went through more changes. My daughter Kabatalya Ateenyi began teaching at nearby schools. She also had a new baby, her youngest daughter called "Katuubi" with Empaako of Atwoki. This baby was also given the name of Amooti. Up to now, I have no idea why the parents decided to name this child twice. My son and his family also returned from Bwamba. He and his wife brought back with them a son and a set of twin girls. The family settled very far away from us in a village called Kiremeezi. There they found land where they could farm and raise their family.

Daughter Herena Amooti also came back from the village of Mbuzi where she was married. She brought with her a son called Nyakoojo with a baptism name of Leo and Empaako of Amooti. By the time the two arrived in Burungu, Byaruhanga had already married, with his own home. He also had two sons. Aliganyira had moved to Kampala City and had found a good job there.

Daughter Herena Amooti did not stay long with us. She bought a piece of land in the direction leading to her brother's home. This was in a village called "Rwensenene" which means: "Place of Grasshoppers." She built her own home and turned the barren land into a productive one. Like her older sister Katalina Akiiki, Herena Amooti was nicknamed a tractor. Her fields always yielded plenty. She had enough food to feed her family and sold some at the market to buy necessities including sugar, salt, soap and paraffin. She even gave some food to her struggling neighbors.

The farming skills that Herena Amooti possessed, coupled with knowledge of herbs and her ability to take care of pregnancies made her a very popular person. She had her own niche just as her younger sister was well-known for excellent teaching and later, her political engagement. Herena Amooti was also a very spiritual person, blending her Christian faith with her understanding of nature. Whenever she was asked about how she knew which plant cured which illness, her response was always:"The plants speak to me."

My oldest daughter Katalina died two years after her younger sister moved to Rwensenene. She suffered from frequent seizures whose cause was not known. One day when in the fields, she fell to the ground and died. This was very sad news for me and my entire family. I did not want to out-live my children. I cried endlessly and was almost inconsolable. As a result, I withdrew pretty much from public life. Even the pre-independence activities did not interest me much.

In 1961, a year before Uganda's independence, Herena and Tinkasimire decided to travel to Congo in search for their father. At first, I hesitated to let them go, fearing

GRANDMOTHER'S STORY

that they too might never return to me. One Sunday after mass, I visited my father-in-law and shared the idea with him. Without any hesitation, he allowed them to go. The only requirement was for them to go visit him and receive a blessing. After the blessing, the two set off for the journey whose details I never received. All they told me was that they had some traders in their company who were their guides.

After being gone for six months, my son and daughter came back and delivered news that their father had died several decades earlier. They had even visited his grave at his fellow trader's home. The cause of his death was Malaria. Since no other trader visited this particular area, there was no way to send us the sad news.

Upon receiving the news, I wailed out loud as though my husband's death had just occurred. My dream of ever seeing him again completely vanished. When my son and daughter delivered the news to the family in Kinyamasika, the entire village and beyond were overcome with immense pain. There was also a sense of relief to know what had happened to our loved one. We organized two last funeral rites, one in Kinyamasika and the other in Burungu. All our children, grandchildren and some other relatives shaved off some or all of their hair. In both villages, there was a big feast.

During the days leading to independence, people had all kinds of ideas about this precious period. Some pictured themselves growing wings and flying up high just like those foreign planes, "enyonyi" (birds) that hovered over their heads. Others, less extreme in their thinking, imagined that they would get free sugar and meat to feed their families. Those without adequate land imagined a time to acquire a lot of land, farm and get rich.

While pondering independence, there were those people who thought they would get cars but worried about how to drive them. Although the wish list was long, the people were happy to simply be free. They continuously repeated the word Independence in different languages. The most common ones included: Uhuru (Swahili); Kwerema (Rutooro); Kwetegyeka (Runyankole) and Kwefuga (Luganda). They also sang songs with the theme of freedom. They pictured the foreigners who ruled them gone forever.

My daughter Kabatalya Ateenyi found her own political voice. She often had long and heated debates regarding the presidential candidates. These debates involved both men and women. Some men with modern ways of thinking enjoyed listening to her ideas. They welcomed her into their company. Deep inside, I knew she had inherited my behavior of having courage and standing up for her convictions. I wished my daughter could also one day, run for the position of President .

Although I did not vote in the elections, I experienced the jolly mood in the country. School children marched in parades and music was everywhere. Free food was served to whoever wanted it. From the sub-county level to the district office, there was plenty of food. I walked to the local trading center to watch the festivities. I watched my own granddaughter Kabagarama march in the parade with her school-mates. With many other people, I waved the national flag of colors black, yellow and red.

Ateenyi taught us how to sing the National Anthem. Even though I was not fluent in English, she made sure I learned how to sing it.

The first stanza of the Uganda National Anthem states:
> Oh, Uganda May God uphold thee.
> We lay our future in thy hand;
> United, free, for Liberty;
> together we'll always stand.

During these times of change, I remained resigned to myself and my small circle of friends. Instead of attending mass at Virika Parish, I prayed at the local village church on a regular basis. I often went with Kabagarama and we sat on the floor covered by obugara which is dry grass from papyrus. This was our carpet. Only the teacher sat on a wooden bench.

My daughter and I often argued over small things. I tried to hold on to tradition, while she worked hard to adopt modern ways. One day, we argued over a cough tablet. I had a cough and Ateenyi sent Kabagarama to the local trading center to buy two cough tablets. When she brought the tablets home, my daughter unwrapped one of them and gave it to me to chew. It was extremely bitter. When she moved away, I got the tablet out of my mouth and threw it away.

When I threw the tablet out of my mouth, it landed on the hen that we called "Kajeru" who was taking care of her chicks. The cough tablet got stuck in Kajeru's feathers. When evening came and the chickens gathered in their shed, Ateenyi noticed something odd in Kajeru's feathers. Upon getting closer, she noticed that it was the tablet that was supposed to cure my cough. She got very upset with me because I had thrown away medicine that had cost her a lot of money. The following day, I asked Kabagarama to get me "Omweya" so that I could chew it to cure my cough. This leaf worked wonders. I instantly recovered from the cough.

Two years following Independence, Kabagarama left home for boarding school. She attended St. Anne Junior School for two years. This was close to our home. For the next four years, she attended secondary school or ordinary level at Maryhill High School in Ankole district. At that time, higher education was still designed according to the British system. Even the very comprehensive exams that the students had to pass were set and graded at Cambridge. During holiday time that lasted one month, Kabagaram returned home. I was always very happy to see her. I prepared her favorite dish of millet and dry mushroom soup called "obutuzi."

Some local boys from the nearby village tried to impress Kabagarama by speaking all the English words that they knew. Whether the words made sense together or not, they spoke them, anyway. One day, she told me that a boy named Makuru (News) who was a local comedian had said; "Yes, it is because, bizagazi, mabingo mahembe kwemyoora." For sure, this sentence made no sense.

Simply translated, it says: "Yes, it is because, grass, reeds, twisted horns." Even though it made no sense, the young man constantly repeated it.

Makuru's friend, called Sabiiti (Born on Sunday) said: "Leave the girl alone. Her grandmother talks directly to God and her mother can read. She can also ride a bicycle and whistle. If you keep on bothering this girl, she will pour out her own rain of foreign words. The words will cause you to get into a trance that will throw you on the ground." The young man took his friend's words seriously. Since then, he never tried to impress my granddaughter with his foreign language tricks again.

Once Kabagarama left for boarding school, her relationship with the family members and villagers changed. Whenever she returned home for the holidays, she was treated as a special guest. She even got her own room in the front section of the house. This room had been occupied by her cousin Byaruhanga who now owned his own home. Her older sister Kajumba occupied the room that was formerly occupied by Aliganyira who had moved to Kampala, the capital city.

Many village women viewed Kabagarama as a very courageous person. They often asked her how she managed to live with the nuns from across the seas. They also wondered how she had learned to speak foreign tongues. What worried some women of the village most was the likelihood that Kabagarama was eating chicken, eggs and fish. One day when we were walking home from church, a neighbor asked her: "Have you eaten chicken yet?" Her worry was that eating chicken, eggs and fish would turn the lovely girl into a bird of some sort. She would lose her decency.

When Kabagarama was asked the question, instead of saying "Yes," she responded in this manner, "aaaaaaa------ummmm---------." She covered her mouth with her hand and politely looked on the side, not daring to look directly into the lady's eyes. From Kabagarama's response, the lady concluded that our wonderful girl had at least tasted the foods that were not okay for a good girl to eat. She turned to me with a suspicious look, placed the back side of her hand on her chin and hummed a song.

The few days that Kabagarama and I spent together during the holidays were very special. We did a lot of singing and praying. My constant words to her were, "Do not ever get consumed by things of this world, my child." I was getting physically weak. I no longer went up- hill to the local church or to the fields. From my bedroom, I went outside to warm myself in the sun. Ateenyi kept on telling me the political news and feeding me on my millet and favorite sauce called "eteke." She also gave me an up-date on family matters. Whenever I missed my Kabagarama, I covered myself with the suuka (shawl) that she had just bought for me. She got the money from her job as an office manager in town. This was her job during the holidays.

As I became increasingly weak physically, I worried about my granddaughter returning home and finding me gone. Although I tried hard to hide my fears, they were real. As many of my contemporaries began to pass away, reality set in for me. I knew that I would never live forever. I found my strength in God. I was also confident that the child that had "fallen on my hand" would never forget my instructions I had no doubt that she would always remember our family story. Whenever she came home, I told her to never forget "Rwabudongo."

WHERE DID MY PEOPLE GO?

BIDDING FAREWELL

Mukaaka passed away in 1971, the same year Idi Amin overthrew the Uganda government in a military coup. I was in higher school (A-level) about to sit for the comprehensive examinations before entering university. Higher school is two years following four years of ordinary level high school. This is the period when students go through preparations for university education. I attended Nabbingo High School, located a few miles away from Kampala City.

I remember occasionally feeling restless and experiencing tingling in the upper lids of my eyes. Although I worried that something was wrong with Mukaaka, I dismissed the idea. I attributed my anxiety and the tingling in my eyelids to worry about the examinations. In my culture, the tingling in the upper eyelid is an indication that something not so good is about to happen. We call this condition "Ekicuro."

The examinations were sent to us from Cambridge. After taking them, we were sent home for the holidays. I rode on the bus from Kampala, the capital city to Fort Portal my home town. When I arrived home, I found people waiting for me. They were wailing to announce that Mukaaka, my best friend had passed away. Mother came running toward me, apologizing for not having told me. Her explanation was that she worried I would not pass the examinations if I knew that Mukaaka had departed from us. Mother assured me that Mukaaka had been buried in her white suit that I had just bought for her.

I surprised everyone present by saying that I knew Mukaaka was gone. I told them that changes had come to my body to give me the warning. We call this feeling: "Kubikirwa." Instead of joining in the wailing, I started praying and singing church songs. I sang the song "Guma, Guma; Yezu Niyo Mpeera", Mukaaka's favorite hymn. I assured everyone that Mukaaka had joined the angels and we had nothing to worry about.

I remained strong because of the Christian faith that Mukaaka taught me about life here on earth being temporary. At death, the soul leaves the body to join God while the body returns to the earth where it came from. This gave me comfort that Mukaaka and I would be together again in joy and peace. This reunion would take place later on after my work here on earth is done.

Another reason why Mukaaka's death did not break me was because she had left me with a treasure. She had deposited in me her life story from which our strong family had sprung. I knew I had important work to do. Now that I knew how to write, I felt equipped to do the work that was left with me. I also felt glad that Mukaaka had lived a long, happy and productive life. Being a survivor's granddaughter made me feel strong, special and unique.

I also did not want to see Mukaaka in constant pain and anguish. I had lived with her during her best days. She had already demonstrated great success in all her work. Her legacy was already established and unquestionable. As I saw her in a state of helplessness, I felt extreme sadness. I was glad she was finally at rest, in heaven.

I came to terms with Mukaaka's departure and continued with my life. Occasionally, she paid me a visit through dreams and visions. With the passing of time, she came less frequently. As I pursued studies, career and started raising my own family, I never forgot my assignment from Mukaaka. Even when I migrated from Uganda to the United States eleven years after her departure, the two of us never parted company.

When Mukaaka revealed her story to me, she was in her 60s. Now in my 60s, I am sharing this story with my family and the world. Talking of miracles, they do exist. This is not coincidence. I call it God's plan, a divine destiny. During the Christmas season of 2017, I decided to do the impossible. I made the choice to move Mukaaka from her resting place in Burungu to Nyabukara Village, our current home.

The decision to rebury Mukaaka was brought about by several factors. First, I felt that she was alone, as though abandoned by the family. Our home had been destroyed and the family had moved away. Another family currently lives on the land. The thought of my precious grandmother sharing space with farm animals such as goats and cattle made me very restless and caused me immense pain. I did not want these animals to walk over her grave. I felt it was my responsibility to move her to a proper burial place so that she could join the rest of the family, particularly her last-born-daughter, Kabatalya, my mother.

Mama Ateenyi Kabatalya, January 2006

Another reason why I felt the urge to rebury Mukaaka was that I wanted to make her story current and her resting place visible. I felt this "Wonder Woman" needed a significant monument. Whoever wants to go and pay respects can go and recognize the physical location where to find her. I wanted to honor, respect and bestow dignity on my beloved Elder.

Mukaaka was a real person who lived in real time. I did not want her life to be made into fiction or to be completely forgotten. On the academic front, I wanted

Mukaaka's story to be part and parcel of the history and politics of Tooro, Uganda, Africa and the World. I am convinced that humanity benefits when we recognize and value all of us. I also want to show the significant role African women have played in shaping African and World history.

Finally, I wanted to rebury Mukaaka because I was not present at her departure in 1971. I felt that it was my responsibility to give back to her what she deserves. I was sure this action would give me peace. I felt obliged to "dress her up" more elegantly and to anoint her body afresh with perfume. Actions speak louder than words. In this act, I am simply saying, "Thank you for what you did for me." She gave life to me and to many others. When I look at my own children and grandchildren, I know they would not be here if Grandmother had not made it possible for me to survive and to thrive.

Mr. Richard Byaruhanga Atwoki

During the Christmas Season of 2017, I spoke to Mr.

Richard Byaruhanga Atwoki, my nephew about what had been on my mind since the year 2011. I wanted him to begin the process of exhuming Mukaaka's body and move her to her final resting place with other family members. Without any hesitation, the young man responded, "Nitukikora" meaning "We can do it." His positive response gave me the strength to move ahead with the task.

The second step in the process was for Richard Byaruhanga to pay a visit to Mrs. Olive Kabururu Kairumba Abwoli, who was ninety-six years old then. She is the wife of the late Mr. Joseph Kairumba who gave Mukaaka part of the king's land where I grew up. When Richard Byaruhanga arrived at the Kairumba home with the request to move Mukaaka from Burungu to Nyabukara, Mrs Kairumba granted him permission.

Mrs. Olive Kairumba Abwoli

After Richard Byaruhanga told me that he had the permission to move Mukaaka from Burungu to Nyabukara, I immediately thought of the next step.

Lillian Kairumba Adyeri

Kairumba Adyeri and Akiiki Kabagarama

Robert Tumwesige

I decided to share the idea with Lillian Kairumba Carvalho Adyeri, one of the Kairumba children who resides in Kentucky, USA. She and I grew up together in Burungu Village. Although she is a few years younger than I am, we pretty much share similar memories of Burungu, Tooro and Uganda.

Upon sharing the idea with Adyeri Lillian, she came on board. She immediately put together an exploratory team that embarked on the project.

Mr. and Mrs. Mawenu *Rev. and Mrs. Musana*

The Team members included a student called Robert Tumwesige who gave me a call on my way back to Kansas after the Christmas vacation in Atlanta. He announced to me that he was joining the team.

The other team members were Mr. and Mrs. Charles Mawenu, Pastor Joram and Mrs. Musana. My nephew, Reverend Stephen Mwesige and his wife Julie Abwoli also joined the team. Mrs. Abwoli Sele joined the team later. She currently lives in Burungu Village. The Team coordinator was Mr. Byaruhanga Atwoki and his wife Tusiime Beatrice Amooti. There were other family members who were not able to be present physically. These include my sister Katuubi Beatrice Amooti, nephew Bamuturaki Mugagga Apuuli and niece Kobusiinge.

After assembling the team, I wrote a letter to the local

GRANDMOTHER'S STORY

Rev. and Mrs. Mwesige *Mrs. Abwoli Sele*

administrators and police department requesting permission to transfer Mukaaka from Burungu to Nyabukara. Permission was granted and the work began. When the team members met in Burungu in search of Mukaaka's resting place, it was almost impossible to find the location. The area was all bush, fields and a banana plantation, with no house in place. There was no stone to mark her grave.

The Search Team

Mrs. Abigaba

Although I described vividly to the team where Mukaaka's resting place was in relation to the house, the team had no idea what I was talking about. None of them was old enough to know what took place in 1971. Most of them were not yet born. As frustration mounted, I thought of one lady by the name of Mrs. Abigaba who was present at Mukaaka's funeral in 1971. Her mother was one of those village elders that raised me. Mrs. Abigaba was invited to join the team. She led them to the area that they were searching for.

Upon finding Mukaaka's resting place, Adyeri Lillian instructed the team to start digging around an area of approximately twenty feet by twenty feet. She also provided very important information regarding the steps to follow in order to get to the actual grave. First, the diggers had to walk around the marked area, piercing the soil using a long, sharp rod. The area with soft soil would be an indication that the soil had been dug up before.

The next step involved digging deep into the soft soil. Seeing a mixture of red and black soil provided the clue that

The red and black soil

the grave had been found. The original diggers must have had to dig a grave that was at least six feet deep. In the process, they threw red soil to the top that got mixed with the darker soil.

Adyeri Lillian continued her wise instruction by saying that reaching the red soil was the clear indication that the body would soon be in sight. After carefully following her instructions, the diggers found Mukaaka's body.

From my home in Wichita, Kansas, I followed every step via WhatsApp. I received the necessary information that was accompanied by photographs. Mind you, I had refused to follow the WhatsApp crowd for a long time. I am now a follower!!

The actual process of starting to search for Mukaaka's resting place in Burungu, ending with laying her to rest in Nyabukara took less than two weeks. There were other people with different skills who joined the original team. They included diggers, builders of the fence, guards, and others who had training in mortuary science. There were also experts in re-constructing the grave so that ladders could be placed along the sides for the workers to go up and down.

Mukaaka's Resting Place

Bidding Farewell

The team did the exhuming work at night with light being provided by battery-operated generators. During the same night, she was transported to Nyabukara and laid to rest before day-break. There is a cultural belief which says that an Elder who had "seen" the sun before should not see it again. On January 21st, 2018, family, friends and members of the community gathered to bid Mukaaka farewell. A fresh church service was held in her honor. May her soul rest in eternal peace.

There are several people who provided key information regarding Palace culture and the history of Tooro. Reverend Canon Rubaale Araali spoke about the battle of Rwabudongo. He testified to have seen Mukaaka face-to-face.

Celebration   *Celebration*

There are other people from Tooro who conducted research and served as consultants for this special project. These include: Mr. Charles Muhanga Araali, Chief Advisor to the King; Reverend Richard Baguma Adyeeri, Mugizi W' Omukama; Mr. Charles Mawenu and Reverend Joram Musana who was also the chief photographer.

Reverend Canon Rubaale Araali

APPENDIX: SETTING THE CONTEXT

The Context of this story is Tooro, western Uganda. A land-locked country, Uganda is located in the eastern part of Africa. The country has a population of 38,787,000 (2018 est.) and occupies a surface area of 93,263 square miles. Uganda's neighbors include the Democratic Republic of Congo to the west; Kenya to the east; South Sudan to the north, Tanzania to the south and Rwanda to the south-west. Uganda obtained political independence from Britain on October 9, 1962.

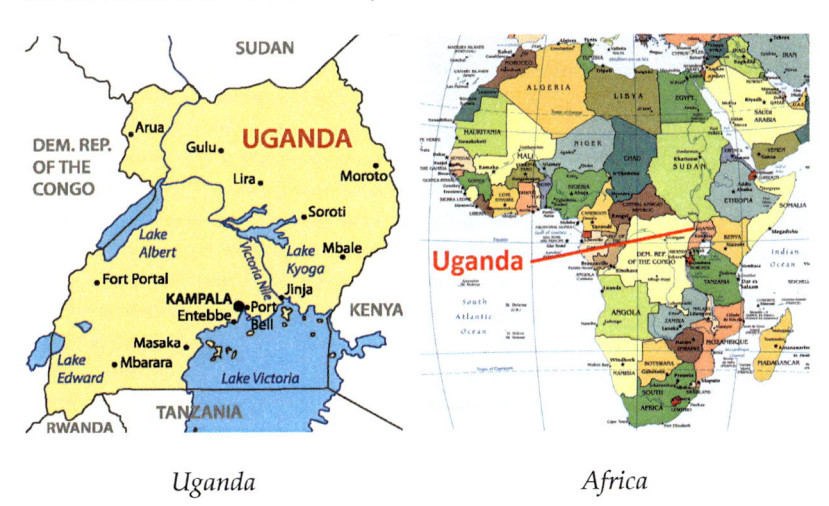

Uganda *Africa*

The flag of Uganda has stripes of black, yellow and red colors. Black represents the color of the people and yellow the color of sunshine. Red stands for brotherhood and sisterhood, the people who died in the struggle for freedom. In the center of the flag is the Crested Crane, Uganda's symbol and national bird.

Ugandan Flag

Uganda's current President is Yoweri Kaguta Museveni. The official languages of the country are English and Swahili. The latter unites the country with the neighbors of Kenya and Tanzania. There are many other languages and dialects spoken in the country. The Shilling is Uganda's currency.

Uganda is a beautiful country which has been called a fairy tale. The equator line cuts across this majestic land. The River Nile, Africa's longest river flows from Lake Victoria, Africa's largest freshwater lake. Winston Churchill, during the coloinal era visited Uganda and called the beautiful country, "The Pearl of Africa."

GRANDMOTHER'S STORY

Equator

The country has a varied ecosystem that includes volcanic mountains, densely-forested swamps and rainforests. The rich, fertile soil makes the cultivation of a variety of crops possible. Coffee is well- known as Uganda's chief export. Kamplala, the capital of Uganda has a population of 1,680,800 (2019 est.) people and occupies 7,297 square miles.

Kampala City

113

Tooro Arms

In the western region of Uganda is the Kingdom of Tooro. This is the place where Mukaaka whose story is told in this book was born. She grew up here, raised her family and it is here that she lies in peace. Tooro Kingdom is estimated to have one million people (2002 National Population Census). Tooro Kingdom's districts include: Kabarole, Kamwenge, Kyegegwa and Kyenjojo. The Kingdom of Tooro has an Emblem and a beautiful Anthem.

Fort Portal

Fort Portal

Fort Portal, the seat of Kabarole District and Tooro Kingdom, is 185 miles by road from Kampala City, the Capital of Uganda. Fort Portal, a designated "Tourism City of Uganda," enjoys an elevation of 4,997 feet with an average temperature of 69 °F. The city's population is 46,3000 people (Uganda Bureau of statistics, 2010).

The Palace   *Botanical Gardens*

The most beautiful features around Fort Portal are: The Palace, Botanical Gardens and Lake Kyaninga. A short distance from Fort Portal are the Hot Springs, another major tourist attraction. the Hot Springs, another major tourist attraction.

Lake Kyaninga   *Hot Springs*

Mount Rwenzori, which is popularly-known as the "Mountains of the Moon" is approximately 54.3 km from Fort Portal. This picturesque mountain is a major Uganda's treasure. It has six ranges, with the highest elevation of 16,762 feet. The peaks are separated by deep gorges. Mount Rwenzori is located on the border of Uganda and the Democraic Republic of Congo (DRC). It is snowcapped and its glaciers are the source of the Nile River.

Rwenzori Mountains

The Rwenzori mountain, a range that is seventy-five miles long and forty miles wide was formed around three million years ago. The uplift divided the Paleolake called Obweruka, resulting in the creation of the modern-day African Great Lakes called Albert, Edward and George.

(*Wikipedia, the Free Encycolpedia*)

Kilembe Mines   *Katwe Salt Lake*

Queen Elizabeth National Park    *Queen Elizabeth National Park*

Within the Rwenzori Mountains are Kilembe mines where copper and cobalt are mined. Copper is one of Uganda's major exports. Not far away from this area is Lake Katwe, a source of salt. In this region is also found the well-renowned Queen Elizabeth National Park. Tourists often come from near and far to visit the animals in their natural habitat.

Batooro (plural) are the indigenous people of Tooro. They are of Bantu ethnicity whose language is Rutooro. Their origins are traced back to the Batembuzi (Pioneers) dynasty. Although not much is not known about the Batembuzi, they were surrounded by mystery. They existed at the height of Africa's Bronze Age. They were considered to be the original rulers of the earth (www. Ugandatravelguide.com).

Batembuzi were followed by the Bachwezi dynasty who were the founders of the ancient empire of Kitara. This expansive empire included areas of present-day western and southern Uganda, northern Tanzania, western Kenya and eastern Congo. Like the Batembuzi before them, the Bachwezi were surrounded by mystery. They were almost treated as gods and to the present day, they are worshipped by many clans.

The Muchwezi (singular) of one's mother is considered to be very important, possessing extraordinary healing powers. A common prayer is, "Muchwezi wa Mau njuna" meaning, "Muchwezi of my mother, please help me." Legend has it that Bachwezi did not die. They simply vanished from the face of the earth. Tradiational gods in Tooro, Bunyoro and Buganda carry similar names of Bachwezi such as Ndahura, Mulindwa, Wamara, Kagoro and many more.

Tooro Kingdom descended from the Bachwezi and Babiito dynasties. The first Mubiito (singular) King was Isingoma Mpuga Rukidi I who ruled in the 14th century. To date, there have been thirty-three Babiito kings. There have also been seven princes who for some reason were not referred to as Omukama (King).

The Kingdom of Tooro was founded in 1830 . This is the year when Omukama Kaboyo Kasunsukwanzi Olimi I, the eldest son of Omukama Nyamutukura Kyebambe III of Buuyoro rebelled against his father and established his own kingdom. Tooro Kingdom was incorporated back in 1876 but reasserted its independence in 1891.

As with other kingdoms of Uganda, Tooro was abolished by Milton Obote in 1967 and was reinstated in 1993 by President Yoweri Museveni. The current monarch is

GRANDMOTHER'S STORY

King Rukidi IV and Queen Mother Best Ke

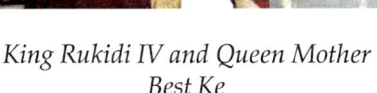

King Rukidi IV

King Rukirabasaija Oyo Nyimba Kabamba Iguru Rukidi IV. He ascended to the throne at three years of age in 1995, following the passing away of his father King Patrick David Matthew Kaboyo Olimi III. According to Tooro tradition, the passing away of a king is called "Kutuuza." The caretakers of the young king include Queen Best Kemigisa Kaboyo and Princess Elizabeth Bagaaya Akiiki. She is Batebe, the king's aunt and his Godmother. President Yoweri Museveni is also one of the caretakers.

Queen Best Kemigisa Kaboyo

Princess Eliizabeth Bagaaya Akiiki

119

The people of Tooro are steeped in a rich culture and traditions. A Mutooro (singular) is expected to be dignified at all times. As a matter of fact, Batooro means, "The Ceremonious Ones." Women are expected to be even more dignified than men.

Batooro are also known for their beauty, gentility in speech, music, love of education and a beautiful, poetic language. Manners and showing respect to others, particularly the elders are taught right from infancy. Batooro work hard to preserve their traditions, are very patriotic, with high self-esteem. One look at a Mutooro and you will see elegance in clothing, uprightness in stature, richness in language and good manners.

Batooro People

Batooro are also very assertive people, often applying the art-form such as music, proverbs, storytelling and

GRANDMOTHER'S STORY

poetry to instilling discipline and enforcing good character. A statement such as "otankwata otanabire" which is translated as, "do not touch me without washing your hands", speaks volumes.

Batooro have a clan system. Every clan has a totem known as "Omuziro" through which members of the clan are related to one another. When a boy meets a girl, they have to announce their clans and those of their mothers at the beginning of the encounter. Unless one is from the royal family, it is taboo for people to marry from their clan or that of their mother. Through this practice, it is not uncommon for people to find relatives outside their bloodline. The totem is usually a non-human part of the environment. Members of a particular clan and those who enter into it through marriage revere their totem and protect it.

Growing up in Tooro, one often hears the statement, "Gira Ak'obuntu" which is translated as, "Have human essence." Batooro teach right from infancy, the importance of preserving their heritage and not to forget their special position of being human. Human principles are taught both directly and indirectly, by example.

Irrespective of one's religious affiliation, Batooro are very spiritual people, portraying strong allegiance to the Creator. Many children's names reflect the power, provision and protection of God. Examples of these include "Byaruhanga," meaning "Everything Belongs to God"; "Kemigisa," meaning "Child of Blessings"; and "Asiimwe" meaning "Thanks be to God."

Tooro's rich cultural heritage is reflected in the ceremonies that take place at Karuziika (The Palace). One such prominent celebration is known as Empango that takes place every year, lasting several days. It is a Coronation Anniversary of the ruling King. For the present King, the date is September 12th. In previous years, this celebration took place twice a year, in Tooro and Bunyoro. It coincided with the harvest seasons and lasted nine days. The joyous ceremony starts with the king sounding the drum which is followed by all sorts of festivities.

Empago, 2019

King Rukidi IV at Empango, 2019

The other prominent ceremony is Amakondere dance which is aimed at entertaining the king. It is led by a royal orchestra that is comprised of well-trained trumpeteers known as "Abakondere." Bark cloth worn over the right shoulder makes the costume. A horn-

Royal Dancers and Drummers

Amakondere Dancers    *Amakondere Dancers*

shaped trumpet, accompanied by drums provide the music. Amakondere dance can sometimes take place in the king's absence. Permission has to be sought. Although this dance is not supposed to take place during sad times, the king can make an exception.

There are other occasions when royal drummers and dancers take center-stage at Karuziika and provide a festive mood. Such occasions include, but are not limited to weddings, religious ceremonies and many more.

Royal Dancers    *Royal Dancers*

WHERE DID MY PEOPLE GO?

EPILOGUE

Thank you for helping me bring my grandmother's story to life. Knowing that someone would pick up this book and read it gave me a good reason to write it. I do not consider you only a reader. I take you to be my close friend and a member of my global village. You are a member of my extended family.

In the pages of this book, you have met words talking about an incredible woman, my grandmother called Mukaaka. Although departed from this earth many years ago, Mukaaka's presence has never departed from me. I can still receive the flavor of her food right here in the living room of my home in Wichita, Kansas. I can also hear her deep voice sing those powerful church and village songs that offer me words of courage, comfort and wisdom. I can picture my grandmother walking through the village, praying for people, settling disputes and administering traditional medicine to heal the sick.

Back in the home where I grew up, I can picture Mukaaka feeding many people, especially children. Her food was very delicious and satisfying. Her pot never ran empty. We ate millet that she stored in her grain store known as "enguli" as well as the new harvest called "omuherya." Millet harvest occurred in the month of December. We welcomed Christmas and the New Year with very delicious millet. There were other crops that Mukaaka planted and harvested. These included sweet potatoes, cassava, maize, green vegetables and beans. We also ate bananas from our banana plantation. When we ran short, Mother bought some for us from neighboring plantations. Mukaaka fed the Village, one of the practices I inherited from her.

I can also picture Mukaaka telling stories around the fire. She made us laugh, since she was a natural comedian. At times, she stood up and danced before us. Talk of evening television shows, we had none and believe me, we never missed them. This is not "sour grapes." We had our own entertainment. I can testify that storytelling is the best form of entertainment and education.

Mukaaka taught me how to enjoy my own company. No wonder I do not feel lonely when I am alone. Remembering Mukaaka's stories, songs, jokes and dances always keeps me entertained. When lost and confused, all I need to do is recall one of her proverbs and I feel alright. When I am lonely or lacking something, I tell myself the proverb; "Ekitaroho tikiriza mwaana" translated as "A child does not cry over something that is not in his/her experience." This proverb gives me comfort and helps me to appreciate what I do have.

I learned how to speak Rutooro, my mother tongue fluently. The type of speech pattern that she taught me is called "Oruhenda" which resembles the name, Kabahenda that she was given at the palace. Many people wonder how I have managed to keep the Rutooro language despite my living away from Tooro for so many years. I believe that whatever Mukaaka planted in me cannot be easily uprooted. No computer can replace her photographic memory.

My mother, being a teacher, instilled in me the technical aspects of Rutooro language. Up to today, I love and have tremendous respect for languages. My grandmother also passed on to me her deep love for nature and for people. It is this deep love for people and all of God's creation that gave me the final reason to write this book.

I am sharing Mukaaka's story at a very interesting stage in my life. When my focus should be on retirement, it seems strange that I am starting again. True, life has a way of giving us surprises. Often when we think we are done, something new, beautiful or even challenging comes our way.

If you are a grandparent, you know what I mean. When you thought you were done with raising your children, the precious grand, great and even great-great grandchildren arrived. With open and loving arms, you started the job of child-rearing again, working from a different angle. I feel that my entire career and life experiences have prepared me well for the bringing forth of this story. This work adds another chapter to my life story.

This book is not only telling a story of a young girl who was orphaned by acts of violence, it is also a call to action. I am sure if Mukaaka was alive today, she would ask all of us to do all we can to end violence. She would plead with us, imploring us to discover the resources that are in, around and about us to create a more peaceful world. She would advise us to live side by side, as brothers and sisters, sharing the abundant resources that the Creator gave us. She would say, "No one should live in constant fear and experience hunger if we all take time to care for one another."

The world has known war for centuries. In our history classes, we study wars that have been fought at home and abroad. Violence has now spread to places of worship, school classrooms, playgrounds, entertainment areas and many other places that once upon a time were considered sacred and sanctuaries to run to in times of trouble. My grandmother's story is a universal phenomenon that is being felt by many people the world over.

Like Mukaaka, many children are daily losing their parents to senseless killings. Parents are also losing their children and extended family members. Other people who once had stable homes are on the run. They are displaced, looking for someone to say to them, "Welcome. You are safe here." Many people spend their lives in jungles, living with wild animals because they have no place to call home. They are running away from fellow human beings who are carrying weapons of destruction instead of food to share.

If Mukaaka was here with me, I wonder how she would respond to my telling her story. Would she congratulate me for being courageous or would she be disappointed in me for exposing her "secret."? Would she ask, "Why did you expose your elders' nakedness?" or would she say, "My Child, I have always known you to be "emanzi" meaning the brave one.

I may not know what Mukaaka's response to my present work might be. I nonetheless know that she would be glad that for all these years, I never forgot what I learned from her when I was a little girl. I also know that she would be glad to see her "little girl" now grown up and having a major impact on the global scene.

I can picture Mukaaka with her hand on her hip, eyes wide open and her neck twisting from side to side, asking "How did you preserve my story for so long?" I am quite sure this would be her simple way of saying, "webale mwaana wange" meaning, "thank you my child." I can also picture my mother, aunts, uncle and the young generation in my family saying, "Webale Akiiki kwegesa. Tusimire. Mukama ayebale." This is translated as, "Thank you Akiiki for teaching. We are grateful. Thanks be to God."

I can hear people of Tooro saying, "You lived in America all these years and never forgot about us and our language?" My simple response would be: "I write and and speak fluent Rutooro because Mukaaka planted it in me." I can also picture students and all peacemakers around the world applauding my efforts because this book offers hope to all of us. When I imagine such responses, plenty of joy runs through my entire being. It also gives me the "Push" to keep moving forward.

I wish you "Obusiinge" which means "Peace."

MUKAAKA'S FAVORITE HYMN

Guma: Be Strong

Chorus	<u>Translation</u>
Guma (x2) Yezu Niyo Mpeera	*Be strong (x2) Jesus is the Reward*
Guma (x2) Yezu Niyo Mpeera	*Be strong (x2) Jesus is the Reward*

1. Yezu Niyo Mpeera — Jesus is the Reward
   Kigambo Ky'okuhiirwa — *This is a Word of Joy*
   Serra h'orakagonza — Search Wherever You Want
   Yezu tainganwa — Jesus has no equal

2. Yezu niyo mpeera — Jesus is the Reward
   Mu bujune muKristu — *When in sorrow, Christian*
   Otaterebukaga — Never be discouraged
   Dorra hali yezu — *Look up to Jesus*

3. Yezu niyo mpeera — Jesus is the Reward
   Nintwarwa Yezu wenka — I am following Jesus alone
   Ekyandagirka nkihikya — I will do whatever he commands
   Ntarukutontoma — Without any complaint

4. Yezu niyo mpeera — Jesus is the Reward
   Obujune buhoire — There is no more Sorrow
   Tulitunga Obusiinge — We shall have Peace
   Munju ya Ruhanga — In God's House